SMALL-GAME SHOOTING

By the same author

BIG-GAME SHOOTING IN UPPER BURMA

WAITING FOR THE BIRD

SMALL-GAME SHOOTING

Experiences of an ordinary Shot

By
LIEUT.-COLONEL
G. P. EVANS, C.B.E.

WITH PEN AND INK SKETCHES BY
IAN GRAY

WARD, LOCK & CO., LIMITED
LONDON AND MELBOURNE

First published . . . 1951

MADE IN GREAT BRITAIN
PRINTED BY JARROLD AND SONS LTD., NORWICH

PREFACE

THIS BOOK PURPORTS to be no more than reflections born of a lengthy experience of shooting. Its pages are not intended for the experienced shot, except in so far as they may serve to bring back to him happy memories of sport with dog and gun —memories of days which may be recalled but can never be repeated, at any rate in their pristine glory.

Rather has it been designed to help in particular two classes of shooters. (1) The youthful aspirant who has been, or is about to be, presented with his first gun; and (2) the man of mature, and possibly of middle, age, who has taken up shooting for the first time, and hopes to make a success of it.

Neither of the above will find elementary instruction in these pages. The A.B.C. of shooting can be found in many books devoted to the subject, although the best mentor is undoubtedly a good coach. But if these reflections have one purpose more than another, it is to advocate a certain independence of action, a desire to experiment until the individual has discovered the method of shooting best suited to his own physical reactions, rather than to follow blindly the precepts of authority on a pastime in which, as in cricket, every man must be a law unto himself, so long as first principles are followed.

It may be objected that I am not consistent in my advocacy; that I have myself quoted an authority, and one of the highest at that. Quite true. I have. But I have nowhere suggested that everyone, or indeed anyone, should follow his advice without finding out whether the methods advocated are suited to himself. Naturally every beginner must learn first principles

—correct stance, presentation, footwork, and so on, but assuming that these have been acquired together with the safe handling of the gun, the burden of my song is to urge experiment and again experiment, until the shooter has evolved the method or methods best suited to varying conditions, and to his own physical and mental capabilities.

For the distribution of woodcock and snipe the following works have been consulted. *British Sporting Birds* (contribution by the Rev. F. C. R. Jourdain), and Hume and Marshall's *The Game-birds of India, Burma, and Ceylon*. For the rest, the source of any quotation is given either in the text, or in a footnote.

"Driven Grouse" has previously appeared in *The Field*, and much of the subject matter of Chapters VI, IX, XVI, and XVII in *The Country Sportsman* from time to time. My acknowledgments are due to the proprietors of these journals for permission to republish in their present form. My thanks are also due to the Editor of *The Field* for permission to quote a paragraph from the Introduction by the late Mr. W. Arkwright to *Spaniels, their breaking for Sport and Field Trials*, and to Messrs. Longmans, Green & Co. for a like courtesy in respect of an extract from the Badminton Library, *Shooting: Moor and Marsh*.

CONTENTS

(Titles appearing in italic refer to verse)

LIST OF PLATES

TO
JACK

CHAPTER I

ON SHOOTING IN SPECTACLES

No ONE WILL CONTEND that glasses are not a handicap in shooting, but except in rain or excessive heat their inconvenience is more imaginary than real. In heavy rain, or even in persistent drizzle, it is well-nigh hopeless to try to shoot in glasses, and if perspiration is dripping on to your spectacles, matters are almost as bad. With rifle in hand, rain or sun is not necessarily fatal to success. The weather may clear, if only temporarily, at the psychological moment, and allow of a shot being taken in favourable circumstances. But fortunately big-game shooting and bad weather do not go together; and whether glasses are worn or not, there is little doing in continuous rain, since the object of your search is usually in hiding.

For the matter of that, small-game shooting and rainy weather do not go kindly together either, but often one has to take the weather as one finds it. When guns and beaters have come from a distance, the shoot has to be proceeded with, for a time at all events, rain or no rain. Uncomfortable as wet weather is to all concerned, guns, beaters, and one may suppose to the game also, it is only now that the bespectacled shooter experiences the essence of discomfort, bodily and mental. Bodily, because in addition to the clammy sensation of raindrops down his neck and up his sleeve, he is entirely blinded by water on his glasses; and mental, because he is the prey of gloomy forebodings which he knows will only too surely be realised. In these conditions it is almost impossible for him to hit a haystack, or indeed even to see one. Added to the mortification of missing is the knowledge that in the eyes of his host, and of the other guns, he will be accounted a hopeless duffer; no consideration being paid to his infirmity, except by such of the party, if any, who share his handicap.

Finally, to make quite certain that his cup of affliction is drained to the dregs, it is precisely when a strong wind is blowing the rain remorselessly on his glasses, that grouse, flying singly and in packs, elect to choose his butt for their line of approach. Coming with the wind at tremendous speed, and well up in the sky, they afford glorious shots—shots which he is quite certain he could bring off with infinite satisfaction to himself if only this qualified rain would stop for ten minutes. Vain hope! The relentless downpour continues. Bird after bird passes his butt within range. He fires a few ineffectual shots without touching a feather, and misery has him for its own. One tiny ray of comfort remains in the knowledge that no one can really shoot well, however good his sight in such weather, and that, therefore, his own misses will not appear so flagrant as they otherwise would. His one hope that an end to this wretched day may now be decided on in view of the hopeless conditions, and that he will shortly be free to forget his woes in the cup that cheers (laced with a generous dollop of whisky) is very likely to be realised, for with drenched and disheartened drivers, shooters enveloped in mackintoshes and wet at that, and with the scarcity of game that always occurs in bad weather, there is little use in continuing to shoot. A halt to the proceedings is usually suggested, and acclaimed by all with one accord.

This admittedly is an extreme case, but such days are within the experience of every shooter. There is, however, a possible remedy for those who are only slightly short-sighted, and that is to dispense with glasses altogether for the time being. Results are sure to be unsatisfactory, but at any rate there is a sporting chance of killing a few birds, whereas with wet glasses there is no chance whatsoever. If the left happens to be the master eye to some extent, and the left lens has been partially obscured, as explained in a subsequent chapter, heavy rain can be defied in some measure by carrying an extra pair of glasses with the left lens made of plain glass, that is without any magnification, and obscured to the correct extent, while the right aperture of the frame is minus a lens altogether, or glasses can be dispensed with, and the left eye closed when aiming. But these alternatives are only possible to those whose sight is slightly below the normal. For the really short-sighted, the only remedy the writer can suggest is to stop shooting altogether until better conditions prevail.

While on the subject of spectacles in the field, it may be as well to take the drawbacks seriatim and so finish with them once for all. Next to rain comes glare. There is no doubt that the effect of the sun's rays is increased when wearing glasses. The obvious remedy, one would suppose, would be to wear tinted glasses. So one can, often with great advantage, when shooting in the tropics. But in the temperate climate of the British Isles one seldom gets a bright sun in a blue sky throughout the day. The natural effect of tinted glasses is to darken everything. Driven grouse creeping over the heather, partridges skimming over the stubble, and snipe darting away a few feet above a background of peat, are hard enough to

13

pick out quickly in the best of light, without the added handicap of bird and background being made several shades darker. Then, as likely as not, in the middle of a drive the sun becomes obscured by clouds, if only for a minute or two. But during that brief spell you may get the very cream of the drive, and find that with your tinted spectacles the birds are almost invisible. I have tried them on driven partridges and on snipe, and found them a failure on both, and consequently never use them now.

Then there is a certain slowness of vision—not necessarily poor sight—apparently inherent in the wearing of glasses, or perhaps it would be more correct to say, in a condition of sight necessitating the use of glasses. The magnification corrects the deficient sight by giving a sufficiently clear definition of distant objects, but it cannot give the quickness of perfect vision. This disadvantage, however, can be overcome to a great extent by experience and concentration. When one knows what to look for and how to look for it, one is in far better case than is the man with perfect sight, but who lacks these two essential qualifications for good shooting.

Having stressed the disadvantages of shooting in glasses I wish I could say something in its favour, but I fear that is impossible. Spectacles *are* a handicap in shooting—there is no getting away from it. But this handicap is only severe in bad weather, and it is seldom, even in the British Isles, except on the west coast of Scotland or Ireland, that we get persistent rain throughout the day, at any rate between August and January. I can only recall, in many years of shooting, three or four occasions when sport had to be stopped for the day owing to bad weather; but a regard for truth constrains me to admit that I have endured many "demd moist unpleasant" minutes in the shooting field, waiting for the clouds to roll by, and the

14

IN THE WORKSHOP

(Facing page 14

THE STEEL PLATE

rain to stop. But there have also been many occasions when brilliant sunshine has retrieved what promised to be a hopeless morning, so perhaps we shooters of the spectacled brigade are not so greatly to be pitied after all.

TO MY SHOOTING SPECTACLES

When grouse are passing overhead
While on your lenses rain is falling,
And temper with the grouse has fled,
My language is, I fear, appalling;

But when the sun comes out to chase
The clouds and halt their erstwhile bluster,
With trembling hands I wipe your face
With pocket-handkerchief or duster,

And put you back upon my nose
With all the haste that I can muster,
The while my face regains repose,
And yours shines with approving lustre.

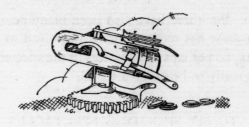

CHAPTER II

ON GUN-FITTING (1)

Chiefly Experimental

BEFORE DISCUSSING GUN-FITTING a word may be said on fitting for rifles. The subject can be dismissed briefly, for the simple reason that there is no real need to be specially fitted for a rifle. Snap-shots are the exception rather than the rule, and since aiming with a rifle is a deliberate process, the eye can accommodate itself to any kind of stock, provided that it is not abnormal in shape. Two things, however, are of the first importance in a rifle—the trigger pulls and the sights. Neither is a subject for theory, but can be determined only by actual trial. The probability is that the short-sighted man aiming through spectacles sees foresight and target clearly defined, but finds the backsight a blur. The writer always had his rifles fitted with a small upright U as a backsight, with an ivory bead foresight, instead of the usual sloping V with a white line down the centre, a form of backsight he found to blur badly. Whatever the form of backsight decided on, it should be placed far enough forward on the barrel to be clearly defined. Lyman or peep sights are useful aids to the short-sighted, and I can testify to the utility of telescopic sights on single-barrel rifles for the shooter in glasses. One does not get quite such a

16

good field of view through a telescopic sight with spectacles as without, since the eye is farther away from the eye-piece. This, however, is of no practical importance, for at the time of aiming the target is visible to the naked eye, and is clearly picked up with the telescopic sight. I have often thought when big-game shooting with open sights, how much I would have liked to try a gold-tipped foresight, such as is sometimes used in America, but I could never manage to get one in England. Both the silver bead and the ivory-tipped foresight are almost invisible when the sun is shining on the rifle, instead of behind it.

If fitting for a rifle is a luxury rather than a necessity, the correct fit of a gun is of the utmost importance, especially to the shooter in glasses. So we will take him first. No one can shoot his best unless his gun fits him, and it should fit the man in spectacles to the proverbial T. So should his spectacles, and, not to put the cart before the horse, let us start with these essential adjuncts to the short-sighted. If he has not done so before, let him go to a first-class oculist and be thoroughly tested. Let him then take the prescription to an equally good optician, having arranged beforehand for a gun—any sort of gun—to be on the premises. He should explain to the optician that he wants the bridge of the frame to be placed much lower down than is usual, because with his head bent down to the stock he will otherwise be looking through the extreme top of the lenses, and may even find himself looking over them. An ocular demonstration with the gun will do more in the way of explanation than a spate of words, and the optician will see at once what is required. I got this tip from a sporting gunmaker who himself shot in glasses, and an exceedingly useful one it is. In due course he receives his perfectly fitting spectacles with large circular pebbles, and with the bridge joining them three

2

quarters of the way down, instead of half way as would otherwise have been the case.

What follows is applicable alike to the shooter in spectacles or without, assuming that neither has previously been fitted for a gun. If money is no object he can go to a leading London gunmaker, order a pair of guns, and be fitted by means of the try-gun and metal discs pulled horizontally and vertically across a white-washed steel plate. Even so, the result may not be entirely satisfactory. His left eye may be found to be the master eye, and he may be advised (a) to have a normal-fitting gun, and to shut his left eye when aiming; (b) to have what is known as a cross-eyed stock—a hideous contraption even when made by a past-master in the art of gun-making; (c) to use a handguard with a raised flap to block out left-eyed vision; (d) to learn to shoot from the left shoulder and to be fitted accordingly; or finally, (e) to have the left lens of his spectacles frosted over to the required extent, to allow of his right eye taking charge when aiming.

It is unlikely that he will get all these alternatives from a single gunmaker, indeed he will be lucky to get the choice of two, but I have been given all this advice by different makers at different times and tried most of them, until I had the luck eventually to strike one who really was a past-master in the art of gun-fitting, and who fixed me up for ever and a day. Until then I couldn't hit a haystack and never knew why, and got so disheartened that I gave up trying to shoot with a gun altogether, and took to big-game shooting instead, which presented no difficulty to my peculiar form of vision.

Although I have no regrets for the good times I have had after big-game in India and Burma, I do deplore the opportunities allowed to slip by in my youthful years of obtaining some of the finest bird-shooting in the world, simply because

I couldn't hit anything. Duck, snipe and quail in the Punjab and United Provinces, various species of pheasant in the Himalayas, *chakor* (hill partridge) in Kashmir, and black partridge—that prince of game-birds—on the Indus in Sind, and elsewhere. Oh dear, oh dear! But there is no use in crying over spilt milk, and I have done my best to make up for wasted opportunities since, not altogether unsuccessfully perhaps.

In the hope that my experiences may be of use to others in like quandary, I propose to speak of them later, but first I must say something on the subject of the master eye. Now, almost any book on shooting that one takes up when treating of eyesight and gun-fitting has a paragraph which reads something like this: "You can easily test for yourself which is the master eye. Point your finger at any small object about ten feet distant keeping both eyes open. Now close the left eye, and note whether the finger has moved appreciably. Now close the right eye keeping the left open, and if your finger appears to have moved appreciably to the right, your right is the master eye." Then follows a perfectly correct scientific explanation of the phenomenon, followed by further details of gun-fitting. Now this test may work out perfectly for most people, but not for all. In my case by this test my right eye is very decidedly the master eye. Actually it is nothing of the kind, at any rate in shooting. In strength of vision my left eye is slightly stronger than my right, but as my glasses are made to give equal vision in each eye, the fact of the left eye being the stronger of the two should not matter in theory. Actually it matters a great deal. When applying the test, my right is equally the master eye, whether the test is made with or without glasses.

In the early days, finding that I could hit nothing that ran or flew and without the slightest inkling of the reason, I tried gun-maker after gunmaker in the hope of a satisfactory outcome. The treatment varied, although the results were uniformly barren. But I will say for these men that mine was a difficult problem, although I was not aware of it, and I am not surprised that they were unable to find a solution.

The first man I went to, after getting me to aim at a stationary mark on the iron plate, made some adjustments to the try-gun, and after a trial or two announced that I was fitted. He was as unaware as I was myself that my left eye was the master, and was easily the worst of the various fitters subsequently tried. It is only fair to say, however, that at that time shooting grounds were not as a general rule fitted with the appliances which later became universal, and which have made gun-fitting a much easier and surer process than formerly. As a final test, he took me to a covered stand behind which an assistant threw easy clay-pigeons over me. The instructor's sole tuition consisted of three words, "Blot it out" which he used with damnable reiteration. That practice was over forty years ago, but I remember it vividly still. I never touched a clay. After about a dozen clays had been sent over me, each accompanied by the usual formula, my instructor began to get quite heated at my invariable miss, and "blot it out" rose at length to a querulous crescendo. My temper was wearing thin too, and gave way at last, and I stopped shooting to tell him quite frankly what I thought about it. He retaliated by saying that if I lived to be a hundred I would never learn to shoot, and that nobody could teach me. We parted after a few more words during which I cancelled the gun I had tentatively ordered, and returned to town to chew the cud of my reflections which were far from happy.

After a few days I tried another maker, and went through

20

the same process with the try-gun which I was beginning to find monotonous. This man must, I think, have discovered that my left eye was the master, but the process whereby he arrived at this conclusion has escaped my memory. His remedy might be termed sweeping. He produced from his pocket a huge black eye-shade and fastened it over my left eye. This, of course, completely shut off everything on the left side, and I felt half-blinded and most uncomfortable. What I looked like I can only surmise. He was coaching another youngster at the same time—in itself an indication of his incapacity—and this horrible shade, and the sensation produced by it, evolved an inferiority complex which completely prevented my paying any attention to his instructions. His last words were to adjure me to wear the shade whenever I went a-shooting. That same evening I wrote to the firm (enclosing the shade) to cancel the order for the gun previously given. Some acrimonious correspondence followed, but in the end the order was duly cancelled, though I recollect that the bill for coaching and cartridges was distinctly on the tall side.

The next man I went to suggested my closing the left eye when aiming. I tried this for some time with a modicum of success, but found it made me dreadfully slow and inclined to poke. It was definitely better than the shade, however, and I could at any rate hit something, sometimes, by this method. However, as I was anxious to learn to shoot properly with both eyes open, I persevered and went to yet another maker who was quite positive that a cross-eyed gun would put me right. Well, he made me one, and a horrible contrivance it was. It was clumsy, badly-balanced, and looked like nothing on earth. And what was worse the butt kept slipping up my arm when mounting the gun, instead of coming into the shoulder. I never hit anything with this gun except by accident, and after

21

enduring it for some months was glad to induce the maker to give me another gun in exchange—needless to say at an enhanced cost—with a normal cast-off.

I then bought a hand-guard with a disc which prevented the left eye from seeing the muzzle of the gun. This was only good for certain shots. It always bothered me, and I soon gave up using it. The reader will not be surprised that by now I was thoroughly disheartened. I could shoot in a fashion by closing the left eye, but when doing so could not get out of the habit of aiming as one would with a rifle, poking badly in fact.

In the end I gave up trying to use a shot-gun at all except for the pot, and after my return to India devoted all my leave to big-game shooting, looking on my gun merely as a useful tool for procuring a camp dinner, mainly by means of the useful if homely pot-shot.

CHAPTER III

ON GUN-FITTING (2)

A Satisfactory Solution

A FEW YEARS LATER I was relating my experiences to a brother officer when he suddenly said, "Look here, you're going home on leave, why not try so and so? He's the best fitter in London, always fitted my guv'nor who swore by him, and fitted me perfectly the last time I was home." "All very well," I replied, "but I can't afford one of his hundred guinea guns" (the price of a "best" gun at the beginning of this century). "That's all right," he said, "Y (mentioning a gunmaker not in the first rank) will fix you up with a sound second-hand gun, and has the use of X's shooting ground (X being the fitter in question), and by arrangement X undertakes to fit all Y's clients when required to do so."

This seemed good enough and I decided to give it a trial. It could do no harm, and if it turned out a failure it would only cost me a pound or so, and leave me where I was. Shortly after getting home I paid a visit to Y, explained matters, and found it was as my friend had said. Y had some nice second-hand guns, and on his recommendation I selected one at a moderate figure, and arranged to try it for pattern at X's ground. If the shooting proved satisfactory, X was then to fit me, but if unable to do so to my satisfaction the gun was to be taken back with only a charge made for fitting, and the use of the grounds. An appointment through Y was made with X, and a day or two later I found myself at the latter's shooting grounds.

We first tried the gun which I shot myself. I had no hesitation about this as I was a respectable rifle shot, and I aimed at a mark deliberately as one would with a rifle. It threw quite a decent pattern—improved cylinder in the right barrel, and about half-choke in the left. After half a dozen shots from each barrel the gun was passed as satisfactory, and then the real test began.

X seemed to divine my trouble straight away. He stood in front of me a few paces distant with his finger on his chin. "Now," he said, "aim at my finger with both eyes open and keep the aim on it until I tell you to take your gun down, and don't close the left eye." He then proceeded to sidestep evenly for perhaps ten or fifteen paces. Then he stopped. "Where is your gun pointing?" he asked. "At your finger," I replied. "Close your left eye," said he. I did so, and lo! my barrels were pointing a good foot to the left. "That's your trouble," said X, "let me have your glasses." Out of his waistcoat pocket he produced some stamp edging and a pair of folding scissors. He cut off a small piece of the paper and stuck it on the top left-hand corner of the left lens. Then we went through the aiming drill again. This time I was only a few inches out. More stamp paper was added, and yet more, until finally I was dead on his finger with both eyes open whichever way he moved. "Now," he said, "get your left glass frosted over to the

24

exact extent of the gummed paper, and you'll do. After that it
will be merely a matter of practice." On examining my glasses
I found that only a segment of the left lens had been covered,
affording comfortable vision with both eyes open, but that
when I covered the right eye I was unable to see the muzzle
of the gun at all.

We now went to the steel plate, and after shots with the try-
gun at the horizontal and vertical moving bird, it was found
that the "cast-off" required was pretty well normal, but that I
needed a good deal of "bend". Having got my correct
measurements we repaired to the tall tower, and there I had a
useful hour's real coaching. X, like many efficient coaches,
was able to see the passage of the shot at 20 yards or so, and,
under his able tuition I succeeded in smashing a fair number of
clays. In due course I received the gun with the stock altered
to my measurements, and took the precaution of having these
measurements put down on paper for subsequent use. I paid
half a dozen more visits to the shooting ground during my
leave, and when I left for India it was in the expectation of
being able to account for a fair proportion of easy chances. I
may add that the partial blocking of the left lens holds good
to-day to exactly the same extent as it did thirty years ago, and
has not been affected by my having had to wear slightly
stronger glasses than formerly.

Of course, this capable diagnosis did not achieve the
impossible. It did not forthwith convert a hopeless performer
into a good or even a moderate shot. Much practice at game
was necessary before I acquired even a tolerable proficiency.
But it did put me on the right path, and thenceforward small-
game shooting became a joy instead of a penance.

This perhaps is the one case in which the shooter in spectacles
has an advantage over the man who shoots without them, and

whose left eye is to a greater or less degree the master. No partial obscuring of the naked eye without glasses is possible. How many shooters whether with or without spectacles, are troubled with the problem which confronted me I have no idea. To such as are, and who do me the honour to read this book I hope that by relating my own experience I may have been able to help them if they have not already arrived at a solution.

Before leaving the subject of gun-fitting a caution is necessary if the stock of a second-hand gun is being altered to the measurements obtained from the try-gun. After being correctly fitted, the shooter should make a note of the measurements required as shown by the try-gun, and should impress on the firm carrying out the alteration that the stock of his gun is to be altered to the exact measurement to the fraction of an inch. A wise precaution before purchasing the gun would be to tell the firm concerned that purchase would entirely depend on whether the gun-stock could be altered without danger of breakage. This seems the obvious course, but many a second-hand gun has been bought without this stipulation to the subsequent disappointment of the purchaser. On receiving the gun after the alteration has been effected, the shooter should not be satisfied with a mere statement of the measurement, but should have the stock measured in his presence, and test the gun on the shooting ground. If there is the slightest discrepancy the process must be repeated, or the shooting will inevitably suffer.

THE MASTER EYE

If your right eye is undoubtedly the master,
  Then everything for you is *right* as rain;
    If the left should be the one,
    Let us hope you're not undone
And are *left* to find the antidote in vain.

But let us hope you find the perfect fitter
  Who will diagnose your trouble straight away,
    And by dexterous provision
    Overcome your faulty vision,
And fix you up for ever and a day.

And if the gun should be a second-hand one,
  Let us hope the alteration will be such
    As can neatly be effected
    In the weapon you've selected,
And that fit and gun will please you very much.

CHAPTER IV

ON CHOOSING A GUN

IF MONEY IS NO OBJECT by far the most satisfactory way of obtaining a gun is to go to a first-class maker and order a "best" gun, or a pair if the shooting obtainable makes it worth while. Before doing so, however, it is advisable to make sure that the gunmaker of one's choice has a fitter who really can fit his clients. Every gunmaker will profess to be able to fit, but past-masters in the art are few and far between.

As in the case of the second-hand gun altered to fit, so here, when the new gun is "in the rough" the prospective purchaser should try it both at discs pulled horizontally and vertically across the white-washed plate, and at clay pigeons representing driven and going-away birds. Any alteration needed can at this stage be easily effected. There is no sense in being put off with anything but a perfect fit. It is for this among other things that the purchaser pays, and he should be satisfied with nothing less. He will previously have stated his requirements, probably in consultation with the gunmaker, as to boring, length of barrels, and weight of trigger-pulls.

But this course will not appeal to the man of moderate means, who has to cut his coat according to his cloth. For him it must either be a cheap gun from a second- or third-rate maker, or a second-hand gun either from a gun-maker, or from a firm specialising in second-hand guns. And if he can find a "best" gun of the required bore and boring, the stock of which fits him, or can be altered to do so, it is a far better investment than a new cheap gun of poor quality. This may throw quite a good pattern, but will inevitably be a clumsy, badly-balanced weapon, in which the owner can take no pride.

The most likely length of barrel to come his way in a second-hand gun will be one of 30 inches. According to modern ideas this measurement is 2 inches too long. But one cannot have everything, and provided the gun is well-balanced, which it is sure to be if of first quality, the extra length, particularly to a tall man, is not of paramount importance. After all, the preceding generation shot consistently with 30-in. barrels and created records that are never likely to be beaten. What is of very great importance, however, is the boring. This should not be too open. For a general purpose gun to be used on driven game and for walking up, a well-distributed improved cylinder pattern from the right barrel with a quarter to half choke in the left should be satisfactory; or in terms of pellets in the 30-in. circle with $1\frac{1}{16}$ oz. of No. 6 shot at 40 yards, say 130–140 from the right barrel, and 150–160 from the left. Should both barrels have a greater degree of choke than this, or even be full choke, it is no disadvantage, and indeed may be all to the good. Choke can always be taken out, but cannot be put in, or at any rate not satisfactorily. Do not have anything to do with a gun with too open a pattern, however satisfactory it may be in other respects. The limit of killing range will be

30 yards, and this defect will be felt when walking up strong well-plumaged game such as duck, or grouse late in the season.

Guns should always be tried for pattern before purchasing, and here it may be said that an evenly distributed pattern is far superior to one with more shot marks in the 30-in. circle, but patchily distributed, of which the "cartwheel" pattern is an example.

As advised in a previous chapter the prospective purchaser will meanwhile have ascertained to what extent the stock can be altered to fit him. If he has not already a record of his measurements he can get these by going to one of the London shooting grounds for this particular purpose. While he is about it he would be well advised to ascertain the trigger-pulls that suit him. This is not a fad. On the contrary it is most essential. Pulls that are too light are dangerous; too heavy are also dangerous, and a fruitful source of missing behind. 4 lb. and $4\frac{1}{2}$ lb. for front and rear triggers respectively are usually considered normal, but these are too heavy for many men. Personally I like 3 lb. for the front trigger, and 4 lb. for the rear, or 3 lb. in a single-trigger gun. The difference is due to the greater leverage of the rear trigger. Here it may be said that the actual weight is not so important as that the pulls should be crisp and clean. A dragging pull is dreadful, and should have no place in a good quality gun. The pulls of try-guns are, for the writer at all events, nearly always on the heavy side.

For those who suffer from a bruised middle finger—often resulting from a bad-fitting gun—the remedy is either a single trigger, or to have the front trigger hung on a hinge so that it moves forward at the recoil from the left barrel. This is

30

quite easily arranged, and the pull of either trigger is in no way affected.

So far, our sportsman (I have to call him by this objectionable name, or by the even worse one of "shooter") has only cursorily examined the gun he thinks of buying. He has felt the weight, ascertained the length of barrels, looked through them, found out the boring, tried the gun for balance, asked the price, and whether the stock could be safely altered to correspond with his measurements. Assuming that the gun meets with his approval generally, and that the price is within his means, the real inspection is to come. The gun should be taken apart, and the barrels suspended vertically by string round the foremost lump, and lightly tapped to see if they give out a clear ring. The inside should be carefully scrutinised for dents—not always easy to see—proof marks examined, and the gun after being put together again held upright by the small of the butt and shaken to detect any looseness. Another and better method is to hold the gun horizontally just in front of the trigger-guard, and to strike the heel of the butt with the other hand when, if the action is loose, a vibration will be felt by the hand grasping stock and barrels. But unless the prospective purchaser is really knowledgeable such tests are best carried out by a friend who is. In any case the maker should always be written to, and the date of manufacture ascertained. Forgeries are not unknown, and the maker's reply will be an additional safeguard. Actually such clumsy forgeries as the engraving of a leading maker's name on a cheap gun are not likely to deceive any but the inexperienced. A "best" gun has quality written all over it, and the fraud would be detected at once.

As to bores, No. 12 continues to hold its place in popularity, and with reason; 16- and 20-bores in good hands may give as good results as 12-bores on driven partridges, but when it comes to high pheasants or duck the superiority of the larger bore is at once apparent. 12-bore cartridges, moreover, are obtainable everywhere; 16- and 20-bore are not. *Raison de plus*.

I have said nothing about prices. A few words on the subject may find their appropriate place here. Gone are the days when a good quality second-hand hammerless ejector could be picked up for a song. Lucky is the man who can find such a gun to-day for £50. £65 or £70 is the more probable figure, and if the gun is a comparatively late model by a leading maker, the owner would have no difficulty in getting £100 for it without its case.

But for rough shooting in Ireland or in the Colonies, a non-ejector hammerless gun or even a hammer gun is for all practical purposes as useful as an ejector, if not quite so convenient. Cheap guns of either, that is guns of poor quality, are simply not worth buying. But plain hammerless guns by good makers are to be had for a comparatively small sum, say £30 or £40, for nowadays there is very little demand for them, and for hammer guns still less. These last even when by leading makers are often to be had for a ten pound note, or even less. They will be old, but if they have been well cared for this matters little.

Messrs. Purdey used to specialise in hammer ejectors— King George V always shot with them—and some of these weapons may still be knocking about. Any sportsman purchasing one of these for a modest sum, if the gun is in good order, and if the stock can be altered to fit him, may consider himself lucky.

A word of warning about the purchase of old guns, apart from consideration of damage from neglect and the ravages of time, may not be out of place. Many of these were built before the introduction of choke. The barrels, therefore, are plain cylinders without any constriction at the muzzle. The boring of such guns is known as "true" cylinder, and owing to a wide spread of shot the killing range is small, 30 yards being about the limit, although the wounding range unfortunately is much greater. These guns do well on driven partridges and near rabbits, but are quite useless for high duck or pheasants with the ordinary game cartridge of $1\frac{1}{16}$ oz. of shot. This should be realised at the time of purchase, and also that it will be very difficult to resell such a gun which may virtually have to be given away.

For those who like ballistics it may be briefly stated that a true cylinder gun will not as a rule average more than 100 pellets of $1\frac{1}{16}$ oz. No. 6 shot in the 30-in. circle at 40 yards, as against 135 or 140 from the improved cylinder, 160–170 from the half choke, and 200–210 from the full choke. But these figures in themselves prove little. Patterns vary enormously, and blown patterns are more commonly met with in true cylinder guns than in any other. In fact, it is the exception rather than the rule, to find evenly-distributed patterns beyond a distance of 30 yards from a true cylinder gun. Improved cylinders show great differences in the density of the pattern thrown, varying from 130 pellets to 160 in the 30-in. circle at 40 yards, according to the boring of that particular gun. As before stated the only safe rule is to see the gun shot for pattern, and preferably to shoot it oneself. If at 40 yards with the charge stated it throws consistently a nice even pattern from well-loaded cartridges, the gun, other things being equal, may be purchased with confidence. I say well-loaded cartridges advisedly, for cartridges can be loaded on the soft side to give a good pattern at the expense of penetration. Such cartridges would be useless on game except at close ranges.

3

To sum up, every shooting man should know approximately the boring he requires, according to the shooting he expects to get. If driven game preponderates, probably improved cylinder boring in both barrels would suit him. But if he is going to have days with high pheasants, or duck, or to walk up grouse, then he will certainly need some choke in his left barrel, and possibly in both. For high birds or rough shooting of any kind, guns with true cylinder barrels are best avoided, for if used the results are certain to be disappointing.

That our ancestors with true cylinder barrels were able to make good bags on walked-up game was due to a variety of causes. A heavy charge of shot, together with a comparatively light charge of black-powder constituted what in these days would be called a low-velocity load. High stubble affording concealment to partridges was left by the scythe, and the tendency of game was to squat rather than to run, so that near shots were the general rule. Then the shooting was invariably over dogs, and more often than not the covey was flushed within ten yards of the shooter. With only half of the present population there were fewer houses and more country; high hedges provided better nesting sites, and the all-important grit was obtainable everywhere, instead of being the rarity it is in these days of macadamised and tarred roads. Cultivation, alternating with copses and rough meadowland, gave partridges the mixed terrain they delight in, so that they were both more widely distributed and tamer, or at any rate easier to approach, than they are to-day. How many of us to-day could obtain a bag of 100 partridges to his own gun by walking up as they did in the days of Osbaldeston, Ross, or Coke of Norfolk?

When we come to driving, the boot is on the other leg. I

am only concerned here to account for the big bags which
were obtained in favourable localities in by-gone days when
shooting over dogs by sportsmen using true cylinder guns,
any other boring being then unknown.

THE QUEST

If you want to have some fun in the choosing of a gun,
   Go search among the shops in gay Mayfair,
      But unless beyond a doubt
      You know your way about
   You'd be well advised to watch your step with care.

You may find the very article to suit you,
   With the balance, fit, and boring you require;
      On the other hand you may
      Fall a victim by the way
   To your ignorance abetted by desire.

For tho' the gun be beautiful to look at,
   It may not be at all the thing for you,
      For it may have too much weight
      Or the stock may be too straight,
   Or the barrels too cylindrically "true".

If money is no object and you seek the easier way,
   Let you hasten to a maker of repute
      Who with deferential air
      Will book your order for a pair,
   And fix you up with everything to suit.

And having once acquired the perfect weapon
   (Whether second-hand or newly built to fit),
      Regard it as a treasure
      To be cherished without measure,
   And do not be induced to part with it.

CHAPTER V

AIMING

THIS SUBJECT BRISTLES with difficulties, the chief of which is that the majority of crack shots are not always certain of what they themselves do, and so cannot tell us. Not that it would help very much if they could, for the personal factor comes in as much in shooting as in cricket, and probably no two men shoot in quite the same way.

To swing or not to swing is the question that crops up annually wherever shooters are gathered together. One man, a good shot, says, "To swing is the only way; any other method is pure chance." Another, equally good, replies in effect, "Nonsense, swinging is a great waste of time; shoot straight at the spot where game and shot will meet." Which is right? Ultimately every shooter must judge for himself, and find the solution for his own difficulties. The trouble is that before he can attain to this desirable end he may suffer much disappointment, and not a little humiliation.

Without wishing to be in any way dogmatic, the writer may perhaps be allowed to give his own opinion for what it may be worth on the two methods, the subject of controversy.

37

I think, then, that both are right, and both are wrong. I think that for all near shots where time is the important factor, interception, or snap-shooting, as some may prefer to call it, is the better way, always provided that the shooter can kill game fairly consistently by this method. It is certainly incomparably quicker, and gives on the whole better results. For high and wide shots where there is plenty of time to swing, swinging is preferable to interception, because of the extreme difficulty in judging the exact spot where game and shot will meet—a difficulty which increases enormously with the distance of the object from the gun.

But let us go to the past-masters of the gun, Lord de Grey, afterwards Marquess of Ripon, and Lord Walsingham—perhaps the greatest shots of all time—and see what they have to say on the subject. All that could be got out of Lord Ripon was the cryptic sentence "Don't check" which obviously refers to swing. One can only surmise that he had in mind wide crossing birds, since for quick shooting he has never been surpassed. As an exception to his usual reticence on his methods of shooting, it is recorded that he once gave a promising young shooter a demonstration of footwork, to the latter's immediate improvement in form. I have always been amused at the late Colonel Cyril Foley's story of how with a view to picking up a tip indirectly, he took the trouble when shooting pheasants at Chatsworth, to go and examine Lord Ripon's footmarks in the snow after the latter had left his stand. These illustrated the demonstration referred to above (which incidentally had not been vouchsafed to himself), for they showed how wide the past-master had moved his left foot to deal with birds passing behind him on that flank, and his right foot for similar shots to his right rear. I shall have more to say on the subject of footwork in a later

38

chapter. Lord Ripon's death from heart failure which occurred during a grouse drive in which he had shot with his usual brilliance strikes one as singularly appropriate to a great shot.

Lord Walsingham writing in the Badminton Library on grouse shooting is more explicit. After speaking of the advantage of shooting with both eyes open he says:[1] "Unless a bird is going straight away he should fly into the shot, and the object is to get it there in time; it will be easily understood that those who put the gun in the right place *by first intention* can do this more rapidly than others who aim first at the bird, and then adjust by swinging forward. A man should know how long it will take him to get ready to fire; and if one yard or two yards of a bird's flight will not give him time to bring his gun to bear, he had better prepare to direct it five or six yards ahead if necessary, so as to get it to his shoulder exactly at the right moment for firing, rather than aim first at the bird or behind it, and then attempt to intercept by following it. In long crossing shots a lateral motion given to the gun may sometimes facilitate shooting well in front; but in this case the lateral motion should be commenced (partly by a turn of the body) in the act of raising the gun; the motion may be continued if found necessary, but for as short a time as possible after it comes to the shoulder and in the act of firing; but it will probably be found that a man who is a good and quick shot will, in grouse driving at least, fire a much larger percentage of shots *without giving any swing to the gun* after it reaches the shoulder than otherwise." (The italics are mine.)

Thus, the greatest shot, with one possible exception, that England has ever known, and the holder of the world's record

[1] *Shooting: Moor and Marsh* (The Badminton Library), pp. 29, 30.

for the biggest individual bag of grouse (1070) in a single day's driving, is clearly in favour of interception without deliberate swing whenever possible. Lord Walsingham's directions—description would perhaps be the better word—for shooting driven grouse have always struck the writer as wholly admirable, so clear are they, so sound, and at the same time so free from dogmatic assertion. Speaking for myself, I find that the closer I adhere to Lord Walsingham's precepts the better I shoot; and the more I swing *when there is no need to swing*, the more likely I am to check my swing, and so shoot behind.

It is commonly supposed that missing or wounding crossing game is chiefly due to insufficient allowance having been given in front; in other words to an error in judging either the pace at which the object is moving, or the distance it was from the gun at the moment of firing, or both. That some misses are due to this cause is certain; but the great majority, I believe, are caused by faulty timing. What happens is this. In racing the bird to get in front, one gets there too soon, or thinks so, waits for the game to catch up, fires, and inevitably shoots behind. One has in fact checked one's swing. This probably is the correct diagnosis of 75 per cent of misses behind.

Why does one wait? Because in rapidly moving the gun in order to outpace the game, the eye is momentarily diverted from the object, and focused on a blank space in the sky. The more distant the game, the greater the space covered by the moving gun. There is nothing to serve as a guide, and the feeling that one has got too far in front is at times almost irresistible, so one checks the swinging movement of the gun for perhaps the hundredth part of a second, and the mischief is done.

40

The only cure probably for this particular fault—short of abandoning swing altogether for the time being—is plenty of shooting. The experience derived from it will at any rate determine the most favourable angle at which to take crossing shots, both when approaching and when going away. The very worst angle is the right-angle, that is to say when a bird is crossing directly in front of the shooter, because of the distance ahead to which it is necessary to direct the aim.

Other faults resulting in missing crossing game are: not giving sufficient lead; incorrect stance; not keeping the cheek down on the stock; tilting the barrels or describing an arc with them—"rainbowing" as it has been graphically called; faulty footwork; aiming too high or too low; dwelling on one's aim, or "poking" as it is called; flinching or jerking as the trigger is pulled; and shooting too far in front—an uncommon fault but not so rare as is generally supposed. All of these except the last, are easily observed and corrected by a good coach, and are soon overcome with practice. Shooting consistently too far ahead is probably due to some slight distortion of vision, and is not easily detected by an onlooker, and is almost impossible of detection by the shooter himself. Many a man has been shooting in front for years under the full impression that he has been missing behind. But once the error is discovered it is quite easily remedied, and is not likely to recur as a habit.

But checking the swing, although the shooter may be, and generally is, quite conscious of the fact, is by no means easily overcome, since it is caused by some discord, however slight, in the working together of hand and eye. Even the best of shots are troubled with it occasionally, if stale or out of sorts. Then we speak of so-and-so as being "out of form", or that he has had an "off day". It takes very little to upset that perfect co-ordination of hand and eye which, as a permanency, is the attribute of the fortunate few, although much practice tends to make it in some degree mechanical.

Probably the best cure for a bout of missing through checking one's swing is a course of interception, the consideration of which may conveniently form the subject of another chapter.

CHAPTER VI

INTERCEPTION

WHAT EXACTLY DO WE MEAN when we speak of interception in relation to shooting? All shooting at crossing game of course is interception, or attempted interception, of a kind, whether we deliberately swing or not. It is an attempt to throw the shot in front so that the game may fly into it. But as used in these pages it is intended to refer solely to shooting directly at the spot where it is expected game and shot will meet, in contra-distinction to the deliberate swing.

If interception, then, is advocated by the highest authority, as we have just seen, as the best method when shooting driven grouse, how much more is it applicable to driven partridges which call for the very quickest shooting, since ordinarily they come into view for the first time as they top the hedge, not more, perhaps, than fifteen yards distant from the line of guns. Quick indeed must be the shot that can account for even one of the feathered bullets before the covey has crossed the line. The second shot will be taken behind the line immediately it is safe to do so, and a rapid change of guns will most likely result in a third bird falling before the covey is out of range. This toll need only be expected from the performance of a first-rate shot.

Now let us consider how a man will fare in precisely similar circumstances who habitually aims by swinging in front of his game, and let us give him the credit for accurate shooting. The most he can hope to kill will be a brace from a compact covey, and he will be fortunate to accomplish this. It is all a question of time. He cannot fire as the birds top the fence, because by the time he has swung in front of his bird it has flown too near the line. This may seem an exaggeration in print, but a little reflection will show that it is by no means so. It does not take long for partridges flying at 40 miles an hour to cover fifteen yards. Actually they are over the line in a flash, and it is all the quickest shot can do to get his gun off in front while it is still safe to do so. Our gun now has to turn round, and, aiming behind the line, to swing in front of his bird and fire. He now has just time, and only just, to take another bird before the covey is out of shot.

Where the slow shot, who need not necessarily be a "poking" one, comes into his own, is when he can stand 30 yards behind a high hedge or a belt of firs, and take the birds as they come over. Here he has plenty of time to swing, and can make sure of one in front, and of another in a crossing or quartering shot, and even of a third if the covey is at all strung out. Or the birds may be so considerate as to come stringing down the front, giving him the chance of bringing off a beautiful right and left, before the depleted covey offers similar chances to guns farther down the line.

Now while we would all like to emulate the quick shot if we could, it is for many of us a physical impossibility. No one can hope to shoot driven game consistently well by interception unless he is quick of sight and possesses a really good eye in the accepted meaning of that term. To the fortunate possessor of this priceless heritage who is taking up shooting whether in his first-youth or later, I would counsel practice and still more practice at intercepting shots until he has learnt the angles at which he can be pretty certain of killing game or breaking clay pigeons. Let him leave deliberate swinging to a later stage, but let him practice snap-shooting as often as he can. When he has discovered that at a certain angle, and at so much forward allowance he can make sure of near shots, such shots will cease to have any terrors for him, and he can go on to more ambitious attempts. Many a first-class cricketer or shot in the making has been ruined as a boy, because he has had stereotyped methods so rammed into him that later he has been unable to free himself from them. They hang as dead weights on aspiring talent.

But what of the rest of us, perhaps in the majority, who cannot hope to emulate these dashing performances? If we go in for driven game we must be content with the one or two birds that we hope will fall to our efforts every time a covey of partridges or a pack of grouse comes within range. And even if we have no "eye" to speak of, there are certain shots which with practice we can bring off by the intercepting method at near grouse taken at a convenient angle.

I say grouse advisedly, because intercepting driven partridges is such quick work, that the man who can only occasionally make use of it with success on grouse is not likely to bring it off under more difficult conditions, particularly as the element of danger is ever present in partridge drives, with low-flying birds and unprotected neighbours on either flank.

But when all is said and done, we go out shooting to please

45

ourselves, and so long as we can satisfy ourselves by our shooting, and are safe and unselfish shots, nothing else matters, and we have every right to enjoy ourselves as the most brilliant performers of them all.

TO SWING OR NOT TO SWING

"Pay your penny, take your choice",
    But it should be your chief endeavour
To hearken to the little voice
    That tells you that it's "now or never".

And let my muse insist on this,
    To shoot betimes tho' no bird fall;
'Tis better far to fire and miss,
    Than be too late to fire at all.

CHAPTER VII

SUNDRY CONSIDERATIONS

IF ONE CONSIDERS the physical make-up of the first-class shots one has known, they will be found almost without exception to possess certain characteristics in common which go far to explain their success. Look at the eyes of any one of them. The probability is that they will be large well-opened eyes, often with a tendency to prominence, in itself not a handsome feature, but nevertheless extremely well adapted for shooting as such an eye admits so much light. It is true that some people with prominent eyes are short-sighted, and have to wear glasses, for which inconsistency, not being an oculist, I do not pretend to account. The lids, too, of your first-class shot will be short, or rather well "hitched up", and indeed may be barely visible. All this means that such eyes are capable of absorbing all the light available, and consequently their possessor will be able to shoot well in a poor light, and to see distinctly grouse skimming over the heather under a darkened sky, when, owing to their plumage so closely toning with the peat and heather of the moor, they would be almost invisible to sight less keen.

48

AT THE SHOOTING GROUND

TURNING BACK

On the other hand, a deep-set eye, especially if heavily lidded, is very unlikely to be a good one for shooting. The entry of light is restricted by the overhanging brows, and is further shut out by blinds in the shape of heavy lids. As to colour, it is unwise for the layman to dogmatise, but I have noticed that a light-blue eye is generally a good one, and green and hazel are also colours not usually associated with poor sight. A full brown eye is often an excellent one, though many very short-sighted people have brown eyes. On the other hand, a dark-blue eye is not generally, so far as my very superficial experience goes, a good colour from the shooting point of view.

I often find myself looking at a man, and saying to myself, "That fellow ought to be a good shot", much as one says, "That looks a good place for snipe." If I myself possessed a good eye it probably wouldn't occur to me to do this. As it is, I get a good deal of amusement from such idle speculations. They don't help me to shoot any better, but they do give me an interest in my fellow man which might otherwise be lacking.

All this is not said in order to fill the indifferent shot with alarm and despondency, and to induce a feeling of inferiority complex. Far from it. But it does, I think, go to show that no one without the keenest sight combined with a really "good eye" need hope to approach the first-class in shooting. It is the quick perception of perfect vision rather than mere long-sightedness which, combined with accurate timing, enables a very small minority to shoot consistently well practically at all times and in all places. But while we give such performers our unstinted admiration, there is no reason why we others should not be perfectly content with, for us, surer if slower methods and smaller results.

4

Footwork

The subject of footwork has hardly been touched on,[1] but is a very necessary part of good shooting. The necessity for pivoting when taking a crossing shot is, of course, widely recognised. By pivoting is meant swinging from the hips instead of moving the upper part of the body only, which is bound to result in a stiffness of movement, and a check to the swing of the gun. In shooting to the right one raises the left heel keeping the right foot firm on the ground as one turns in the direction of the game, and vice versa when shooting to the left. But there are times when this is not enough, and in order to get comfortably round, it is necessary on occasion to move the feet as well. This will generally occur with wide birds, or when an approaching bird on the flank has not been seen in time to take it well in front, or when one has fired at a bird, and turns to deal with another which is passing behind the shooter. When swinging to the left, the left foot should be straddled rearwards and the right heel raised, and vice versa if the game is flying to the right. Some there are who say that the right foot should never be moved in any circumstances, but I fail to see how one can get round comfortably to shoot to the right without moving the right foot.

Anyone can demonstrate this for himself. Let him put up a gun or a stick and swing to his right rear pivoting in the usual manner, but without moving his right foot. See how awkward it feels! He can't get round, he is straining his arms, and his gun is all over the place. Now let him move his right foot just a short pace to the rear. What a difference! He can get round with the utmost ease, and could almost take a bird going away right behind him. So to the left in exactly the same

[1] See Chapter V.

50

way, moving the left foot to the rear and raising the right heel.

It may perhaps be as well to say that the feet should not be moved unless necessary, as of course, it doesn't make for steadiness. When birds can be taken comfortably from the usual stance it should be adhered to, the shooter always "pivoting" if he has to make even a partial turn.

Swing

Since in the minds of some there may be confusion, or at any rate uncertainty, as to what is meant by conscious (or deliberate) and unconscious swing, it may be as well to attempt to define the terms. The first is a deliberate movement of the gun as it races the game in order to outpace it. It is immaterial whether in the first instance the gun was pointed behind, or at, or in front of the object, or whether it was actually swinging when so pointed. The essence of the thing is that the movement to outpace the game has been deliberately and consciously made.

In the unconscious swing, as the gun is brought to the shoulder it is automatically directed in front of the game and fired the moment the butt comes home. This is the only swing imparted to the gun, and it is part and parcel of the movement of the body in the direction of the game made in the act of raising the gun, and not afterwards. In other words it is interception at its best.

FOOTWORK

Now if your stance is easy, yet firm as well as neat,
When shooting to your front there is no need to move the feet;
But when you turn to either flank as birds across you race,
Then pivoting's the only way to shoot without disgrace;
And if you need a wider swing to shoot towards your rear,
Then move your foot a trifle back to swing your body clear;
So shall you shoot in comfort as from the hips you swing,
The while to every movement dexterity you bring.

Now your eyes may be of a hazel green,
 Or a dark and beautiful blue,
But whether you hit 'em, or whether you miss 'em
 'Twill be certainly said of you,
"He may not be very much of a shot,
 But he shoots in capital style"
A trifle to tickle your vanity,
 But it's surely well worth while?
And when you pull 'em out of the sky, and they crash with a sounding
 thud,
It's great to know, as you homeward go, that you've shot as a
 sportsman should.

CHAPTER VIII

GROUSE

THE GROUSE IS SURELY the prince of British game-birds for the sport he gives when driven, walked up, or shot over dogs. The capercailzie and the blackcock may exceed him in size and magnificance, but neither can approach him in numbers, or in the varied forms of sport he provides, nor can any scenery surpass the charm of his surroundings.

I must admit that for me the chief pleasure in shooting grouse over dogs is derived from the scenery and watching the dogs work. A man must indeed be insensible to the beauties of nature who is not exhilarated by the scent of the heather in his nostrils, and the feel of it under his feet, by the wine-like freshness of the air, and the sight of the loch in the far distance shimmering in the sun. I enjoy too, watching the intense expression on the dogs' faces when one or other of them draws up on a warm scent, beautifully backed by his companion—a look of suppressed eagerness that is almost painful in its intensity, until finally the pack springs and the shot is taken. Here

53

for me the pleasure ceases, for I do not shine at going-away birds. If a grouse is good enough to swerve to right or left before passing out of range, so presenting a quartering shot, I may kill it; but your straight going-away bird I detest, and make a mess of more often than not, even when shooting over dogs. As for walking up grouse without dogs, this would have no charms for me, scenery notwithstanding, which shows what an indifferent performer I am at this kind of shooting.

But however good I might be at walked-up birds, whether with or without dogs, driven grouse would always appeal to me more, not because the shots are more difficult, for I often think they are not, but because of the variety at all angles, expected and unexpected, making demands on one's powers of observation, judgment, and experience, which are not exercised in the same way when walking up.

The hardest shot at driven grouse to my mind is when birds come "creeping" over the heather, as it is termed. Only they don't creep. They come very fast, very low and if there are clouds overhead, are sometimes almost invisible, so perfectly does the plumage tone with the background of heather and peat. The only way to deal satisfactorily with such birds, speaking for myself, is to take them far out, say a good fifty yards. They will be well within range by the time the shot reaches them. If one hesitates, hoping to get a clearer view, the chances are that before one can get the gun off they will have arrived at a point at which it would be dangerous to fire. But just because of the difficulty, such shots when successful are very satisfactory, almost as much so as the really high grouse which affords the acme of gratification when brought down, falling as it does with a most satisfying thud twenty yards or more behind, though shot well in front.

54

A peculiarity of flight, common both to partridges and grouse, consists in rapid wing beats interspersed from time to time with the normal skimming flight on outstretched motionless wings. This habit is most disconcerting to the novice, and I remember well how it bothered me when I first began to shoot driven grouse. Its object, doubtless, is to accelerate speed. In all pictures of driven grouse the birds are almost invariably shown skimming on motionless wings, and, indeed, no artist could possibly portray the wing-beats. But the novice knowing nothing of this habit goes by the pictures. In his first drive a pack of grouse comes straight for him, skimming on motionless wings, the birds gently swaying from side to side in the very poetry of motion, exactly as portrayed in Thorburn's pictures. Our novice selects a bird and is just going to fire at it, when it suddenly flaps its wings rapidly half a dozen times and puts him clean off. Unconsciously he thinks "I'll wait till it has finished," but by this time the pack is over his head and is gone. Round he swings and fires two ineffectual barrels at their vanishing forms. As in other matters familiarity breeds, if not contempt, at least indifference, and after a while, knowing what to expect, he hardens his heart and takes his selected bird at the proper distance whether flapping or otherwise. I feel that the word "flap" hardly conveys the action. It implies a slow motion, but not only is the flapping rapid, but the pace is extremely rapid also, and the only thing to do is to fire as soon as the bird comes within shot, regardless of its gymnastics.

One of the most difficult things, I find, to carry out when shooting driven grouse is this business of taking birds sufficiently far out. It sounds so easy. But the tendency is always to wait too long. I have seen it stated in print that grouse are often missed by being fired at when too far off. But I do not think the first contingency often happens, except when the birds have passed the butt, and then alas! long shots are all too common, and not always fired by novices either. It is a tremendous help if there is a conspicuous mark, between fifty and sixty yards out, such as a boulder, or an extra long sprig of heather, or a tuft of grass—anything which catches the eye. It is necessary, of course, to be a fairly good judge of distance, but most shooting men can estimate distance pretty accurately to forty-five yards—the killing limit of the shot-gun if heavily choked—and it is not difficult to guess at another ten yards beyond that distance. But often the friendly boulder is lacking, and the eye searches a sea of short heather in the vain attempt to single out some sort of landmark. One can then only trust to luck and try to remember to take the birds far out, much farther than one would expect to kill them if stationary.

This inclination to wait is occasionally almost irresistible. The birds are sometimes swerving as they come, or flying at a difficult angle, and the rapid wing beats of which I have spoken, help to induce a momentary delay. But I think the real reason one waits is from fear of missing. In another second or two, one argues, they will be within nice range. Fatal delusion! So they will, but once more it is not a case of "the 'and deceiving the h'eye", but the other way about. The pack indeed is within such nice range that as the gun is raised it is already over the shooter, and it will be a lucky toss that brings down one bird, whereas two ought to have been shot in front, and you know it. But like old Father William, "You do it again and again", or at any rate I do.

Of course, the man who intercepts habitually "by first intention" has a pull over the shooter who has to find his bird first, and then throw in front of it, or over the man who has to come behind and race through. The first can afford to let his birds come closer, and still has plenty of time to get off two shots in front. But the fact that he has to take his birds farther out should not in itself present an insuperable difficulty to the slower shooter. He knows that he cannot afford to let a pack come within forty yards before firing at it, and that if he does he cannot hope to bring down more than one bird. He *must* harden his heart, and take birds fifty or sixty yards out, regardless of whether they are easy or difficult, skimming or swerving. The cure, of course, for undue hesitation is plenty of shooting, unfortunately not easy to come by. Still, a lot can be done if a man faces his weakness resolutely, and refrains from making excuses to himself for misses that he knows in his heart were due to one cause only.

Grouse-driving in Ireland differs considerably from the same sport as carried out in Scotland. For this there are at least three good and sufficient reasons. First the scarcity of grouse which in comparison are few, so few indeed, that on a Scottish moor they would be considered negligible. Secondly, grouse are not generally driven in Ireland, but are almost universally shot over dogs. Indeed it is doubtful whether any driving has been attempted in Ireland since the war. And finally, the Irish beater is accustomed to driving woodcock in coverts, and here noise and plenty of it is necessary to prevent the cock sitting tight and breaking back. So when he is enrolled to drive grouse, he adheres to the traditions to which he is accustomed, and which have been practised by his forefathers for generations. Grouse on the wing are saluted with shouts all down the line, rising in crescendo until distant shots inform the beaters that their efforts have been recognised, when the shouting dies away to be replaced by normal conversational tones. Flankers are quite likely to join in the chorus, and will certainly wave their flags ecstatically. Sometimes their zeal has the desired effect. At other times results are not so good, particularly if a wind should happen to be blowing from a flank, and on-coming grouse, not appreciating either the flanker's flag or his objurgations, turn down wind and stream across the front hundreds of yards out of shot, to break out at the opposite flank where all the shooting and waving of flags in the universe isn't going to turn them.

But grouse-driving in Ireland should not be taken too seriously. Everyone is out to enjoy himself, and the newcomer who will certainly find conditions distracting, would be well advised to enter into the spirit of the game, and make light of, shall we say, trifling informalities. The mental attitude of the purist from a Scottish moor would doubtless be similar to that of the Colonel in Bateman's picture of the guardsman "who dropped it". He would do well to keep clear of an Irish grouse moor, or mountain as it is usually termed; but if he wants to see Irish sport at its best, let him take part in a big woodcock shoot, and if he doesn't enjoy himself to the full he must be very hard to please.

Your Irish beater no doubt has his faults, especially when called upon to drive grouse. On the other hand his many good qualities are apt to be overlooked. He is invariably cheerful, no day is too long for him, no ground too rough or too steep to climb, no weather too bad. And he is delighted when good shooting, admittedly under difficult conditions, rewards his efforts to provide sport. The writer has enjoyed too many good days with Irish grouse and Irish beaters to cavil at unorthodox procedure, which in Ireland at least should be taken as part and parcel of the day's fun.

As a substitute for much shooting in the field one is tempted to practise on clay pigeons. But a word of warning is necessary. While with clays one can practise to some extent shots which one finds difficult—one's pet abomination in fact—no clays, however cunningly thrown, can be made to represent driven grouse, for the simple reason that in order to come over or past the shooter at speed, they must be thrown a comparatively short distance from him. In fact, when he sees the clay he must shoot at it. In the nature of things, therefore, this cannot possibly help him to take his birds far out, though it may, and probably will, help him to get his gun off quickly. Driven partridges can be much more successfully imitated than driven grouse, as more often than not one only sees partridges for the first time as they top the fence, and one must shoot on the instant or not at all. There can be no waiting.

I personally think that while an hour's practice with clays, with a good coach to correct mistakes, just before the grouse season opens will help anybody, even the best of shots, almost as much good can be derived from aiming drill at home, provided a man has sufficient experience to know what he should and what he should not do. Ten minutes with his gun every day for a week before shooting begins will work wonders in taking the stiffness out of his arms and shoulders, and in enabling him to bring up the gun on a mark as it comes to the shoulder.

I am definitely of opinion that too much practice in clays is not a good thing for grouse shooting, though excellent for high pheasant. For one thing clays sent over are usually very well defined, whereas grouse very often are not. Also clays may occasionally, but cannot habitually, be sent over in coveys, to say nothing of packs, and it is numbers that confuse. In short, for the reasons given, "driven" clays are very much easier than driven grouse; and in practice it is difficult conditions we need, not easy ones.

DRIVEN GROUSE

When grouse are coming fast and high
   In perfect weather,
Their forms outlined against the sky,
There's time to swing with hand and eye,
And drop a brace as they sweep by,
   Upon the heather.

When grouse are coming fast and low
   And all together,
I know, ah yes, full well I know
That I should take the nearest, so,
And drop two neatly in a row
   Upon the heather.

But do I do it? No! I wait,
   And not a feather
Falls because I hesitate,
Or fire too early or too late,
And only shot in leaden spate
   Drops on the heather.

CHAPTER IX

PARTRIDGES

IF THE GROUSE HEADS the list of British game-birds, the partridge is easily first in popularity. Its ways are charming, and given the slightest encouragement it is a friendly bird, seeking rather than avoiding man's vicinity. It is a devoted mate, the cock bird taking his full share in the rearing of the young, and mothering them entirely when disaster overtakes his helpmate.

I once had a signal instance of this. I had placed some partridge eggs from an exposed nest under a bantam hen. In due course they hatched out, and the bantam used to take the chicks away for the day, always, however, returning at sunset, when she and her brood were driven into a large portable run enclosed by wire-netting. Even after they had reached the "cheeper" stage and could fly quite well, she always brought them back. Just about sunset one would hear a swish of wings and the brood would alight on the lawn, the little bantam having preceded them by a few seconds, sometimes on foot, but often in flight, for she could fly quite strongly for a short distance. One evening the brood failed to return, and there was no sign of the bantam. At last when it was almost dark, the welcome sound of wings was heard, and the covey alighted in the usual place, but the birds were unusually wild, and I had considerable difficulty in driving them into the pen. The bantam was not with them, and it was certain that something had happened to her. Next morning I found the poor little hen dead in a rat-trap. I had enclosed this in a tunnel, safely as I thought, but she had got in, and had tapped the pan with her beak, and been caught by the head. It was some consolation to know that death must have been instantaneous.

Next morning, having scattered food outside the pen, I opened the door in some trepidation. On coming out the birds began to pick up the ants eggs I had provided, and presently took wing as usual, alighting in a rough field below the house. That night it was again dark before they returned, but next morning to my surprise there was a cock partridge outside the pen. He flew off as I approached to open the door, and presently the young partridges flew down to the field as they generally did. That night they failed to return, and I wondered whether disaster had befallen them. But next day I put up the brood from the rough field, and leading them was a fully-grown partridge. At the time I could not be sure that it was my friend of the day before, but subsequently I saw him daily with the brood, and eventually he became quite tame, pecking about with them on the lawn. But it was curious to note how rapidly the call of the wild asserted itself among the brood as soon as the young could fly really strongly. They would take wing at the least alarm, and from the time the cock partridge took them over, they never again returned to roost.

The covey, always led by the old cock, was going well into

62

September, but in October I noticed a depletion in numbers, and it became increasingly difficult to identify the covey as it grew wilder and rose at greater distances. I hope that the old cock at least survived the shooting season, and lived to rear many broods of his own. I may say that the sex of the old bird was never in doubt. Not only had he the usual well-defined horseshoe—generally but not infallibly the hall-mark of the cock partridge—but as he stood on the alert, as he often did, while the adopted brood pecked about and satisfied its appetite, I watched him for minutes together through powerful binoculars which showed up every feather as easily as though I held the bird in my hand. The delicate chestnut pencilling on the scapulars, and on the back of the neck—the most distinguishing mark of the cock partridge to my mind—was clearly visible, while the rich chestnut at the side of the head and on the cheeks also proclaimed the male.

The unselfish devotion of the cock partridge—to use an adjective ordinarily appropriate to human beings—is shown not only when the young are hatched, but during the time the hen is sitting. When she comes off the nest to feed, as she does for a short spell in the early morning, the cock bird acts as sentry until she is satisfied. Standing motionless, with neck stretched to the full, and looking twice his usual height, he remains on the alert, occasionally taking a pace or two, but never relaxing until his mate, having finished her meal, is back again on the nest. Then, for the first time, the cock resumes his normal attitude, pecking about here and there, until he, too, flies off to mount guard, what time "the patient dam assiduous sits". Uncommonly glad he must be, one may suppose, when the downy nestlings at long last break through the shell. Not that his duties are at an end even now. Far from it. He watches over the brood almost as assiduously as the hen, and

63

the pair may often be seen in inclement weather sitting side by side on the nest, with the youngsters tucked away comfortably in the parents' warm feathers.

Then what a brave fight the partridge makes for sheer existence in this modern England of ours! Cut out while on the nest and often mutilated when not killed by the mowing machine, exposed to cold winds and the public gaze from hedges bared almost to the roots, finding oil and tar on the road instead of grit and dusting places, and deprived both of cover and an adequate food supply on stubbles cut almost level with the ground, and overrun with fowls from innumerable chicken farms—the wonder is that partridges manage to exist at all. It is a hard struggle indeed, but the little bird puts up a gallant fight, and in localities suited to its needs continues to show sport. Farmers have long ceased to regard the partridge as a menace on the land. It does nothing but good, and often brings in a substantial rent to the farmer who lets his shooting. Finally, where encouraged it shows magnificent sport, only beaten in this respect by its distant relative the grouse.

Walking up partridges is now a sport of the past in England, although still practised in parts of Scotland and Wales. Partridges are always a welcome concomitant of the rough shoot, but elsewhere they are generally driven. As a sport, driven partridges take a lot of beating, and despite the comparative tameness of the scenery, some men even prefer it to shooting driven grouse; while I know of no sportsman who would not prefer a day's partridge driving to covert shooting, unless, indeed, the pheasants were real "screamers".

Comparisons are not invariably odious, and although it would be profitless to compare driven partridges with grouse—

PAST THE LINE

PARTRIDGES WELL UP

for each form of sport is delightful in its way—we may, I think, touch on the comparative difficulty in shooting. It is generally considered that driven partridges present more difficult shots than do grouse. The reason is not far to seek, or rather the reasons, for there are many. Take the position of the guns in the first place. Instead of being in comfortable butts from which they have a wide field of view, they are stationed, let us say, about fifteen yards behind a hedge just high enough to hide them at this distance, and too thick to see through. Fifteen yards may seem quite a fair distance to the uninitiated. Actually one has barely time to present the gun before the birds are over and past. Then there is the sudden appearance of the covey, always reminding one of a Jack-in-the-box. The birds may flash by in a compact group, or they may swerve and split up on catching sight of the guns. Uncommonly difficult they are, whatever they do. Add to this the danger of firing at low-flying partridges, with guns and loaders unprotected on each side of you, and beaters perhaps drawing near in front, and it becomes evident that shooting driven partridges is no game for the tyro.

Of course there are exceptions. There are times when grouse are as difficult as any partridge. When, for instance, they are skimming low over the heather under a black sky, or when they are swerving in a high wind, or, perhaps hardest of all, when they come over in a large pack of a hundred birds or more, making it difficult in the confusion of numbers to select individual birds to shoot at. Conversely, partridge shooting can on occasion be delightfully easy. When it is possible to stand twenty-five or thirty yards behind a tall hedge or a belt of fir trees, and the birds come high to clear the obstacle, or when a covey is turned by the wind and comes down the line almost in single file, affording lovely individual shots. But

5

take it by and large, driven partridges do, I think, give more difficult shots than grouse. The sudden jink of a frightened partridge is harder to deal with than the more uniform swerve of a grouse. Then the abrupt appearance of the birds, although expected, and the nearness of the shooter to the average hedge tend to make the shooting as difficult as anyone could desire and a great deal too difficult for many of us.

I have already said in Chapter VI that, in my opinion, the most satisfactory way to deal with driven partridges is by interception if the shooter can accomplish it. Speaking for myself, I am resigned now to the knowledge that to attempt to intercept driven partridges is for me merely to waste cartridges. I can do it occasionally with near grouse, and have no doubt I could do it sometimes with partridges too, if—and this is the crux of the matter—I knew beforehand exactly where they would appear. With grouse there is nearly always visibility for at least fifty yards, and most likely for five hundred. So all you have to do is to bang at the estimated distance in front of the bird when it comes within range, and you either get it or don't. But with partridges the covey may come to the right or left of you, or straight over. So you cannot face in preparation for, say, a quick shot to the right. Now, given the necessary experience and practice, the better the sight, the quicker as a rule will be the reaction to things as they are—in this case the sudden appearance of the covey. The shooter with exceptional sight sees it a fraction of a second before his less gifted neighbour, and has turned in the required direction, and got his gun off almost before the adjacent gun has realised that the birds are there. This is not to say that the latter is exceptionally slow; it may only mean that the other is exceptionally quick. But the effect is the same—two shots to the other's one.

66

For a long time Stuart-Wortley's advice[1] on shooting by intercepting worried me badly. In spite of all warning to the contrary—and every shooting coach I ever met deprecates this method and is insistent on swing—I felt instinctively that he was right, and my own observation of the action of first-class shots confirmed it. Where I went wrong was in thinking that because I *ought* to do it I *could* do it, if only I had sufficient practice. So I practised on clays in desultory fashion with indifferent success. I found it was very difficult to get them thrown aright. I could intercept successfully sometimes, when I knew how they were coming, but when I had them thrown haphazard they were nearly always either too high or too wide. And, of course, I tried on partridges, too, at great self-sacrifice; for it was dreadful to court an almost certain miss, when I knew that I could account for at least one bird in a covey by different methods. Gradually it dawned on me that it was not so much a question of practice as of eyesight, and this realisation brought great comfort. Now I don't bother. I swing in front as quickly and as steadily as I can, as soon as it is safe to do so, and if, as is usually the case, I am close to the hedge, I drop my bird (assuming the shot to have been successful) by a quartering shot behind the line. My second barrel will then be at a bird from the remainder of the covey as it is going straight away, and if I have the good fortune to bag it also, I am grateful for the favour the gods have shown me.

When shooting at driven partridges and standing pretty close to the hedge, there is one shot which I devoutly hope will not come my way. It does, of course, in my turn, as it does to everybody. The shot I mean is when a covey, or a single bird for that matter, comes low over the hedge straight for you and nearly takes your cap off. The very quickest of shots can hardly

[1] *The Partridge* (Fur and Feather Series), p. 105.

get his gun off in time to take such a bird in front. For myself, I wheel round and endeavour to put paid to its account by firing at its tail. As I have said before, I don't shine at these shots, and two ineffectual barrels are sometimes followed, I fear, by an over-loud malediction which floats unseemly on my neighbour's ear.

One is sometimes tempted to move a few paces to the right or left to avoid an obstruction, such as a tree growing in the hedge. But it is generally wiser to stay where one is. By moving one probably gets too close to the next gun, and too far from the gun on the other side. Besides, the tree may prove a blessing in disguise, as the covey will be diverted by it, and will pass on one side or the other, thus affording a side shot if high, and a quartering shot if low, either of which should result in a kill.

The ideal distance is from twenty-five to thirty yards from a really high hedge or a belt of firs, and it is very noticeable how much larger a toll is taken from the coveys when the guns are so placed. Here one has ample time to swing and to take two birds in front, though one certainly, and possibly both, will fall behind the line. How delightful it is in these circumstances to stand on firm turf, and to feel that your footwork is not hampered by sticky plough, and that you can swing freely in any direction without the slightest danger to anyone. And how satisfying when in answer to your right-and-left two little round balls come hurtling to earth, killed as neatly as anyone could wish! Alas, except in a few favoured localities, such ideal positions are few and far between, and if they occur twice in a day's driving and the birds are plentiful, one may consider oneself blessed beyond the ordinary.

Another good position, and not too frequently found, is where one is able to stand right up against a low fence, and shoot over it at the oncoming partridges. These give very interesting shots, as one can take them far out, but one must be careful to hold low enough, for the birds do not rise to clear the fence until they are almost on it. In these positions one is often hampered by a ditch on the shooter's side making foot-work impossible, and also by the advancing beaters, but the first birds to be flushed by them can at any rate be safely shot at.

It is this habit of partridges to skim low between the hedges that makes the shooting so difficult. If they habitually flew at a sufficient height to clear the hedge in front of them, behind which, all unsuspected by them, the guns are waiting, partridge-shooting would be shorn of half its difficulties, for the birds would be visible for ten or twenty yards before they topped the hedge. But they are much too wise to do anything so foolish. They skim across the field a few feet only from the ground, and as they get close to the hedge, up they pop like so many Jacks-in-the-box, and are gone before one can say "Jack Robinson". No wonder they are hard to hit! And so one feels doubly pleased when able to defeat their knavish tricks, either by standing thirty yards behind a thick fir belt, or up against a low hedge and shooting at low-skimming partridges before they have time to put their popping tactics into execution. Poor little birds, they have a hard time of it; but if there were no shooting there would be no preservation; and without the killing off of vermin, the partridge as a British bird would soon be as extinct as the Dodo.

Here I feel I must say a few words on behalf of the French partridge. It is rather the custom to pooh-pooh the good qualities of "red legs", but I notice no one declines to shoot him when they get the chance. I own to a decided liking for the "Frenchman", not because he is an easier bird to shoot than the brown partridge—although I am not sure that that isn't a point in his favour—but because he comes so manfully to the guns. No dodging tactics for him! Straight as a die he comes, disdaining all subterfuge, and as he is twice the size of the British bird and usually flying singly, he generally meets a warrior's death. But the "Frenchman" has one virtue which should endear him to all sportsmen. Unlike his cousin of England, he does not remain in a covey when alarmed. He makes use of his legs, and as the beaters approach, the covey splits up, each member of it running to right and left before the advancing line. Consequently when forced to rise they distribute themselves along the line of guns, thus affording shots to most of the shooters, instead of only to one or two, as does a covey of brown partridges when skimming by in a compact mass.

Time was, not so long ago, when the French partridge was looked upon as vermin by sportsmen and keepers, but especially by keepers, who went out of their way to put a heavy foot on a nest of eggs when found. This was in the days of shooting over dogs, and even much later, but before the era of driving, when the good qualities of the "Frenchman" began to be appreciated. Keepers declared, not without reason, that the red-legs demoralised the dogs by running before them, and the English birds, by communicating to the latter their evil ways. They also accused the French bird, most unjustly, of aggressive habits, and declared that they drove the English birds away from nesting sites, and ate their eggs! Indeed, there was no end to the wicked propensities of this much maligned bird. As everyone knows now, the boot is on the other leg. The French partridge is a quiet peaceable bird, not in the least a bully, and is driven away without hesitation by its fiery little congener, when the latter has decided on a nesting site and the

French bird is in the vicinity. This Hitler-like aggression is practised by an old pair of brown partridges which drive off all others intent on nesting, whether of their own or other species. Young birds are much more peaceable, and it is not uncommon to find nests of both species close to each other in the same hedge. As for accusing the poor "Frenchman" of eating the other's eggs, it is an egregious libel which could only have originated from ignorance or spite, on the principle of giving a dog a bad name and hanging him forthwith.

I have seen too many indifferent days of partridge driving in East Anglia redeemed by the "Frenchman", when English birds were few in number, not to give him his due; and he has afforded me, personally, such excellent sport, that I should be an ingrate indeed not to feel kindly disposed towards him. May I in return be allowed to put in a plea on his behalf? The French partridge is a biggish bird, the size of a grouse, and about as tough as an old cock grouse—to kill, I mean, not to eat. Please, then, do not take long shots at him when he is going away. The chances are that he will carry on as though untouched, only to die a miserable death three or four fields away, or more likely to fall a victim that night to prowling vermin. Long shots at any going away game is a reprehensible practice, often indulged in, to their shame, by good shots; but the French partridge should be placed in the same category as the hare, and, unless approaching or crossing, should not be shot at beyond thirty yards.

I always feel that in England the fine flying qualities of the French partridge do not receive the recognition that is their due. Indeed, owing to its habits and habitat, it cannot display them to full advantage.

The red-legged partridge of the Himalayas, known to all Indian sportsmen as the *chakor*, is so close a relative of the

"Frenchman" that unless the two species were examined closely together, not one man in a hundred could tell by looking at it whether the bird he held in his hand was a *chakor*, or the French partridge of Europe. The *chakor* is perhaps slightly the heavier bird of the two, and there is a slight difference in the plumage of the throat, but otherwise the two species are indistinguishable by the sportsman. But the *chakor* is a bird of the mountains, and affects the stony precipices of the Himalayas. A brute to run, it is a grand bird to fly; and when dislodged from its fastnesses by a motley crowd of hillmen who have climbed to a position of vantage before dawn, it provides sport of the highest order, giving most sporting and difficult chances, as the coveys hug the hillside just like grouse, or launch themselves across a valley a thousand feet and more below them, making for the precipices on the opposite side. If the two species could change places I have not the slightest doubt that the sedate "Frenchman", as we know him, would sustain the reputation of the *chakor* for fast and dashing flight; while the magnificent speed of the *chakor* would of necessity give place to the slower and straightforward flight of the European bird. It is almost entirely a question of habitat. We see much the same thing here in England in the pheasant put up fifty yards from the guns from a Norfolk copse, and the same species flushed from a hilltop in Devonshire at a distance of several hundred yards, and free-wheeling at terrific speed over the guns standing in the valley below.

Not that the French partridge is a slow flier—on the contrary it has a strong dashing flight—but from its habit of running until forced to take wing, it rises as a rule too near the line to really get up speed before reaching the guns. The brown partridge, on the other hand, keeps united if possible, and squats rather than runs, in roots at any rate: consequently

72

the covey is easily flushed and comes to the guns at top speed.

The little brown bird has a big place in my affections, as it has in those of most shooting men. All the same, if I owned a partridge shoot in the Eastern Counties, I should not feel happy unless there was a good sprinkling of "red legs" on the ground.

PARTRIDGE DRIVING

The guns behind the hedge are lined,
Each on his shooting stick reclined:
The sky is blue, October's air
Is keen enough the blood to stir;
Now with suppressed exhilaration,
Each muses in anticipation.

But hark! the keeper's whistle blows,
Bringing us upon our toes:
Moments now will surely settle
Whether we are men of mettle . . .
Every fibre braced to feel
Ready eye and nerves of steel.

An interminable wait
Follows, seconds charged with fate;
Faint again the whistle from
Afar, then whir! . . . a bursting bomb
Of partridges with eldritch sound
Is right and left, and all around.

Now for instant calculation!
Now for quick deliberation!
Bang! and bang! and down there falls
One or two small bouncing balls,
Changing guns with swift design
You drop one more behind the line.

That's the way beyond a doubt,
The only way to blot 'em out,
Shooting as they come in view,
No time now to follow through;
Interception true but quick,
Cool and steady does the trick.

Callous it may sound, no doubt,
To write of "blotting" birdies out;
To praise the skill as each one falls,
And talk of feathered "bouncing balls";
But, please, in self-extenuation
Let me give an explanation.

First, in driving thanks to pace
'Tis kill or miss the usual case;
Wounded birds it can be seen
With decent shots are few between:
A poorish shot 'tis safe to say
Will hardly hit a bird all day.

Ban shooting, and you'd shortly see
Partridges would cease to be:
Vermin free from all control
Of sitting birds would take their toll;
Snares and nets, and poachers' skill
Would take a larger number still.

Eggs for search by rat or crow,
Nests despoiled by midnight foe;
Shots by poachers slinking round
At coveys jugging on the ground;
Harryings without cessation
Would shortly spell extermination.

That sport is cruel in some degree
I must reluctantly agree:
But Nature "red in tooth and claw"
Bears out the universal law
(Prevailing in the Wild for all)
Which sends the weaker to the wall.

Why do we shoot? Because the skill
Involved gives each of us a thrill:
Because the feel of wind and weather
With exercise, combined together
With Autumn scenes and tints divine
Stir the blood like generous wine.

With minds at rest we shoot with zeal,
Tho' mindful of the birds' own weal;
The increase in our partridge stocks
Explains this seeming paradox;
No shooting and no preservation . . .
And the next step's extermination!

So here's a health to sportsmen true,
To keepers, flankers, drivers too;
But first we'll toss a bumper down
To hail the little bird in brown:
May he increase and thrive in flocks,
Our sporting little Jack-in-box.

CHAPTER X

PHEASANTS AND COVERT-SHOOTING (1)

ALTHOUGH THE PHEASANT has been naturalised in Great Britain from, it is said, the eleventh century or even earlier, it is still regarded as more or less of an alien. This is not due so much to the fact that its original habitat was in Asia Minor, as from its many crossings with allied species from China and Japan effected in recent years. The Old English Black-neck (*Phasianus colchicus*), the original pheasant of Great Britain and Europe, is now a rarity, so much have the different varieties crossed with each other; and even among so-called wild pheasants nearly every cock will be found to have the white ring on the neck more or less developed, true indication of Chinese or Mongolian blood.

While it would be outside the scope of this book to describe the different varieties of pheasant reared as game-birds on game-farms and large estates, a brief mention may be made of the varieties which chiefly concern the sportsman at any rate in covert-shooting. These are: (1) The Old English Black-neck

77

(*P. colchicus*). The original pheasant of Great Britain, and possibly indigenous. Now rarely met with, although a few game-farms make a speciality of rearing this bird separately, or did before the war, and keeping it as pure as it is possible to keep birds that interbreed so freely. This is comparatively a small pheasant, a very gamey-looking bird, hardy, and a good flier. (2) The Chinese pheasant or Ring-neck (*P. torquatus*). A compact bird, rather larger than the Black-neck, also a good flier when forced to use its wings. (3) The Mongolian pheasant (*P. mongolicus*). The largest of all our pheasants—a very handsome bird with a deeper white ring than the Chinese pheasant, and white wing coverts. A heavy bird, and not so good a flier as either of the first two. (4) The Japanese pheasant (*P. versicolor*). A lovely bird of a dark bronze colour. I have had no experience of this bird when covert-shooting, and only remember to have seen it on game-farms.

In addition to these, and now becoming common, is a species which first cropped up some fifty years ago. This pheasant, so far as is known, is not a cross but was bred from pheasants in our woods and aviaries. It is known as the "Melanistic Mutant" (*P. tenebrosus*) and is very dark in colour. The hen of this species looks rather like the grey hen of black game. It is said to breed true to type. The "Melanistic" is quite hardy, but in my experience is not a good flier. Although I have seen a good deal of this species I have only shot it in Bedfordshire and East Anglia—flat country where it is difficult to show good birds. What sort of show the Melanistic Mutant would put up if pushed off a high hill in Devonshire or Wales I am not prepared to say. But I do know that among several really high birds that have come my way in other counties, I never yet saw *P. tenebrosus*, although it was sometimes quite common in that particular covert. Consequently, I am not

78

enamoured of this bird, in spite of his handsome appearance. All the pheasant tribe, of course, prefer to use their legs rather than their wings, but when forced to take to the latter from a distance some put up a much better performance than others. The lighter the pheasant the better as a rule it flies, and the hens for this reason usually fly higher than the cocks.

If I were rearing pheasants I would endeavour to get eggs either from the Old English Black-neck strain, or from a cross between *P. colchicus* and the Chinese bird, or failing that, from the Chinese Ring-neck (*P. torquatus*) entirely. I would eschew the Mongolian—although I have seen this species fly well—because its weight tends to keep it low, and if too liberally fed it rapidly puts on weight, and no fat pheasant *can* fly well. The Japanese pheasant I do not know, and the Melanistic Mutant I would not have at any price.

As to the wild pheasant, it is nearly always a cross between *P. colchicus* and *P. torquatus* or *P. mongolicus*, and a truly wild bird it is as regards its habits and mode of life. Actually it is the descendant of pheasants reared for covert-shooting a few generations back. But there is nothing of the tame about it, and it takes a sportsman shooting alone all his time, even with a good dog, to outwit a cunning old cock. With head held low and looking half its size it starts running (and it *can* run), half a mile away, and unless the dog has nose and pace, and his master can run too, the bird is more than likely to make good its escape. If, however, it can be induced to take cover in a patch of brambles or a thick hedge, it should prove a gift for the gun.

It is not bad fun for two active sportsmen with a couple of well-broken spaniels, and a man or two to help, to work along a thick hedge, or small copse, in the endeavour to track the wily "rocketer" to his lair. It is a healthy and a cheery game, as

79

one works from copse to copse, and from copse to hedge, with the spaniels' stumpy flags wagging vigorously in the ecstasy of excitement, culminating in joyous yelps when a rabbit is afoot. The bag will be small, and the shooting rather tame, though now and again a pheasant may give a decent shot, and the shots at rabbits will at any rate be sporting ones. But generally speaking, the pheasants will not be really extended, and as often as not will only afford a snap-shot at close range through the trees, which must be taken on the instant, or not at all. At other times a long raking shot will be given, as the wily bird, having run to the end of the hedge or covert, sneaks out at a corner, and takes wing only a yard or so above the ground. Unsatisfactory shots, these, when the pheasant is likely to be winged, and a long stern chase ensues. Let us hope, however, that the dog catches the bird before it reaches the cover it is making for, and brings it back in triumph.

It may not be the highest form of sport, but it is a healthy and very pleasurable form of exercise, and a grand means of acquiring woodcraft and a bump of locality. Small wonder that our ancestors loved it, since their only weapons were flint-lock and percussion muzzle-loaders, and covert-shooting as we understand the term to-day was unknown. A pheasant was a pheasant in those days, and a triumph when brought to bag, as well it might be, considering the unwieldy weapon that brought it down, and that every pheasant was a wild one in every sense of the word.

Covert-shooting as practised before the war was no doubt artificial to some extent in so far as the pheasants for the most part were reared under fowls, and were fed and tended with a great deal more care than is bestowed on farmyard chickens. But when actually shooting, the artificial nature of the sport should in no way be apparent, if the pheasants are

80

shot at the proper time of year, and are shown in a proper manner. Your hand-reared pheasant flies just as strongly as the wild bird, and from its flight it is impossible to tell it—or it should be—from a pheasant that has never known a keeper's fostering care, but has had to acquire wisdom in the hard school of nature, as its parents and grandparents did before it.

Covert-shooting can be glorious sport, or it can be disappointing, depending almost entirely on how the birds are brought to the guns. Woodland scenery makes its own appeal; and although the glory of autumn is past—since pheasants should not be shot until the leaf is off the trees—the delicate tracery of birch and beech, and the stouter branches of oak and ash, against a November sky, have a charm of their own, enhanced by the russet carpet of fallen leaves with which the wood is plentifully bestrewn. There is a shrewd bite in the air despite a bright sun in a blue sky flecked with fleecy clouds.

Expectation of good sport runs high, as seated on your shooting-stick you try to anticipate how the birds will come. There is no sense of artificiality here. All your thoughts are centred on the prospect of sport and the only doubts that assail you, when the shooting is well managed, are concerned with your ability to pull down the tall birds that will presently be sailing over the tree-tops.

Before discussing coverts in flat country, let me recall one of several happy pheasant shoots in which I had the good fortune to take part in Devonshire. Our host was a sportsman of the old type. A good, but by no means a brilliant shot, he was extremely unselfish, always putting himself in the worst place, and never so happy as when providing the best of sport for his guests. Little rearing was done; for the most part the birds were wild, but wild or tame, high birds were the order of the

6

day. The guns would be placed in a valley, sometimes lining a road, at others on the opposite side of a deep combe, and again at the foot of a steep field on the bank of a trout stream dancing over the boulders, and making merry music on its way to join the parent river. But always towering above one was the high hillside, covered with trees of every description, in which oak perhaps predominated. Meanwhile, the beaters have climbed the hill by a circuitous path, and have formed line below the crest on the opposite side, the object being to flush the birds as far from the guns as possible. Now the voices of the men can be faintly heard as they shout objurgations at the spaniels, of which there are always some with beaters in Devonshire. Almost at the same moment the first birds, and the best, come into view. So high are they that it is difficult to distinguish cocks from hens, the latter flying highest of all. Sailing on motionless wings and apparently flying slowly, they are actually moving at high speed, and it takes a good gun and a good man behind it, to make consistently good practice at these top-sawyers.

Now the beaters show here and there among the trees on the sky-line, and begin to move down the hill. There is very little noise, for the head keeper, a Devonshire man, is well versed in the ways of both pheasants and beaters, and has them well in hand. Easier birds now come off the hill in twos and threes, easier, but none too easy for all that. They are still nearer forty than thirty yards high, and come over well above the trees, and are going all out. You take the first bird, a splendid old cock, and, as he sails over you, you throw the gun well in front of him, and down he comes, crashing in the bracken thirty yards behind. You swing on to a hen rapidly approaching, and even higher than the cock, and put paid to her account also. Another bird comes over while you are reloading and gets away

82

unshot at. Then you get a glorious shot at a cock which has come down the line far out, and has already had four barrels at him. You miss him with the right, but to your joy crumple him up with your left just before he becomes your right-hand neighbour's bird. You were under him with your right barrel, and make a mental note to hold a little above a wide-crossing bird. Then you miss a cock and get another hen, and suddenly there is a shout from the beaters of "mark 'cock, mark 'cock" which tells you that a woodcock is on the wing. You catch a glimpse of the bird well to your left as it swerves through the trees, and the report of three barrels comes to your ear. Your host, you know, is on the left of the line, and if the last barrel was his, the probability is that the cock is his also. You get two or three more shots, all good birds, and bag a cock, missing the others completely, and the beat is over, and the beaters, dishevelled but cheery, make their appearance.

It has been a good drive, well carried out, and the shooting has been satisfactory. For your part you have fired a dozen shots or so, and have five birds down, and not a runner among them, all good birds, and two at least real "screamers", and you proceed to collect them in blissful content, assisted by an under-keeper with a good dog, for the birds have fallen for the most part in tall bracken. Your five birds which, incidentally, ought to have been eight, are, in your eyes at least, worth fifty of the "miserable critturs" you sometimes see pushed reluctantly out of cover to rise almost at your toes. Your host, by the way, shot the woodcock all right after it had been missed with both barrels by the gun on his right, who got difficult chances as the bird jinked through the trees. And so the day goes on with varying fortunes, but with every bird a good one, and the majority very good. The actual bag was

83

never large; a hundred to a hundred and fifty for the first time over to six or seven guns, if the shooting was respectable, with perhaps three or four woodcock to add variety to the bag. Compared with the totals of pheasants shot on big estates, before the war, running into four figures in a day's covert-shooting, the results of this shoot and of others like it may seem pitifully meagre, but it is quality that counts, and in that respect this small shoot was second to none.

One of these good birds was nearly responsible for my being mulcted in damages for destruction of public property. A long wood was being beaten on high ground and of the guns, six in number, two walked with the beaters, two were at the end of the wood on a high bank overlooking a road, and two others were on the road itself, on each side of the small railway station which flanked it. I was on the bank just above the road, and presently a high and wide cock-pheasant came sailing over the trees with intent to cross road and river, and to make for a wood some hundreds of yards beyond. He was swinging with the wind as he passed me—a real nasty shot, but all the luck was on my side, and I got him fair and square. He crashed with terrific velocity into the station wall, missing the large station lamp by inches. My luck was doubly in, for had he hit it it must have been smashed to smithereens, and it would have cost me five pounds at least to make good the damage. The shot was a lucky fluke. I happened to get him just at the right angle of his curve when I might so easily have missed him. But it afforded me a satisfaction out of all proportion to its merits. The two guns in the road who were preparing to shoot the bird if I missed it, could not have been as pleased as I was. I can only hope that I had the grace to suppress the elation which was inwardly consuming me.

It is always interesting, I think, to hear how others shoot, and here is my own method of taking high birds. Whether it is the best, or even the usual method I am not prepared or qualified to say. I only know that it is the only way for me, that is, when I manage to hit high birds at all. If the bird is coming straight overhead or towards my right front, I take a short step backwards with my right foot, at the same time slightly bending my left knee, and keeping the ball of the left foot on the ground for the sake of balance. This has a faint suggestion of the attitude of a dancing master, but it throws all the weight of the body on the right leg which is what is wanted, thus enabling one to get well back. I look hard at the advancing bird, and when it is about a gun length short of the perpendicular throw up the gun pointing just behind the tail, and without pause race it rapidly through until the bird is completely blotted out. The trigger is then immediately pressed with the gun still swinging. By this time the bird is exactly over one, and if the manœuvre has been correctly carried out the probability is that it crashes to earth, shot in the neck and head. If, however, there is the slightest check the bird flies on untouched. In the case of a high bird approaching on my left front the procedure is exactly the same with one important exception. Instead of coming up behind the tail, I bring up the gun behind the outside tip of the left wing, and fire when the wing is blotted out. The reason for this is that since the gun is pointing across one's body the shot will be "low left" if the bird itself is aimed at. I got this tip many years ago from a good coach, and it has been worth many a high bird to me. In the case of a smaller bird, such as a high grouse or partridge, I try to miss the left wing entirely by shooting just clear of it, to the right.

One would suppose that the same principle would hold good when shooting at a bird on one's right front, but it doesn't—

with me at all events. I try to blot out the body just as I would if the bird were coming straight over me, and if there has been no check I expect to get my bird.

I find that while I can sometimes kill high grouse or partridge when taking them far out, I fail signally if I try to do this with pheasants or duck. I suppose it is the denser plumage of the larger bird that protects it; also, no doubt, the greater strength of breast and wing bones. To make certain of either, I must get my bird overhead, when the shot penetrates through the feathers, rather than strikes against them. Low pheasants or duck, of course, are just as easily killed in front as when overhead.

To shoot a high bird of any kind that has already passed over the shooter, and for which one has to turn round, the only way is to intercept it. The late Charles Lancaster in his book *The Art of Shooting* written some fifty years ago, calls this an easy shot "because the bird is never lost to view". This is the only instance, I think, in which I find myself in complete disagreement with the author of that most excellent treatise. To me, and I think to most men, it is a most difficult shot, as it is so "chancy", and calls for such accurate timing. All interception is difficult, but it is very much easier to throw the shot where you think it will meet an approaching bird, than it is when the same bird is going away from you. And the higher it is the harder it is to judge how far in front to aim.

I think I could count on the fingers of one hand the times I have successfully intercepted birds going away from me. One I remember was a duck, not a particularly high bird, and no one was more astonished to see it come down than I was. Another time I brought down dead as mutton by this shot a really high pheasant. I had attempted to take the bird—a hen —well out, and though I was not conscious of having made a bad shot, the bird was apparently untouched. I spun round, and as the pheasant sailed away well past me by now, I allowed what appeared to me to be ten or twelve feet in front of it and pressed the trigger, aiming, of course, underneath to throw the shot in front. To my surprise the bird doubled up and came crashing down in a thicket, from which it was retrieved with difficulty. It had, I remember, a couple of pellets underneath the chin, and was apparently untouched elsewhere.

It so happened that this was the only good bird of a wretched day, in which the birds were not only few and far between, but miserably low, being driven out of a huge wood into the arms of the shooters assembled outside. What induced my adventurous bird to rise of its own accord, as it must have done at the far end of the wood, and to come sailing over our heads well above the trees I do not know, but I do know that the bird was seen only by the gun on my right and by myself, and that as the former had not waited to watch the result of the left barrel, not a soul other than myself saw the lucky shot. So I got very little satisfaction out of it, which was as much as I deserved for a fluke of the first water.

THE FREE-WHEELER
(or Bobby's novitiate)

Over the trees, over the trees,
Here comes a cock pheasant helped on by the breeze;
  On motionless wings he seems to glide,
  As his body sways gently from side to side;
Tho' he's up in the sky over ninety feet high,
When he reaches my stand he'll most certainly die
  (Unless some despicable son of a gun
  Shoots him first, and so selfishly settles my fun).

Over the trees, over the trees,
He's out in the open as high as you please;
  His neck is outstretched and so is his tail,
  And he looks rather like a fine ship in full sail;
But tho' a tall bird, its really absurd
To miss him as Jones has, for hark! 'pon my word!
  "Bang", "bang", go his barrels in rapid succession,
  But the pheasant sails on in his stately progression.

Over the trees, over the trees,
He's left them behind and he's out on the leas;
  Smith, Johnson, and Brown have banged off all together,
  And haven't succeeded in touching a feather!
Now glory be! He's coming to me—
I can't miss a mark that's so easy to see;
  I'll wait till he's properly over my head
  In order to bring him down perfectly dead.

Over the trees, over the trees
He's over and past me before I can squeeze
  A trigger or even throw forward the gun,
  I'm properly diddled before I've begun!

I try to crane back, but alas and alack!
Catch my foot in a stump and come down with a whack,
  And I know as I ruefully pick myself up
  That a free-wheeling pheasant has "sold me a pup!"

Under the trees, under the trees
I sit in despair with my head in my knees:
  I've missed a high pheasant—*the* bird of the season,
  A heaven-sent chance—but that isn't the reason
I'm sick with despair and sit holding my hair,
For I've boasted and bragged and—my best girl was there!
  Mirth-stricken she stood disregarding my moans,
  Now she's gone to laugh over my sorrows with Jones!

CHAPTER XI

PHEASANTS AND COVERT-SHOOTING (2)

Good and Bad Birds

IT IS WELL KNOWN that if pheasants are forced to fly where they do not want to they will either give low and unsporting shots, or endeavour to break back—a manœuvre they generally execute with success. Advantage can be taken of this trait by putting stops just outside the covert with instructions to keep up a low tapping, and also to show themselves through the trees. The result will be that the birds having been gently pushed to the end of the covert will be most reluctant to face the mysterious tapping, and still less the figures that have shown themselves here and there. Instead of coming forward, they will rise and fly back over the tops of the trees, giving most sporting shots to guns placed far back in the wood. It will help matters if wire-netting or similar obstacle be placed in a clearing twenty yards or so from the end of the covert to make them rise, where they will have room to clear the trees. Otherwise a certain number might sneak out at the sides. The driving of course, has to be very carefully done, and for the last part the bulk of the beaters should be halted, and the keeper with two or three experienced assistants should alone go forward, in order to flush the birds in twos and threes instead of in numbers as would otherwise be the case.

How different is an arrangement such as the above, from a procedure which was still quite common before the war in which the guns were collected in a field just outside the covert, or along a ride in a big wood. The birds that broke back did so with impunity, for there was no one to shoot them. Those that came forward crossed the ride a few feet above the heads of the guns, or sneaked out across the field at the sides, if they possibly could, flying a few feet only above the ground. What sport can there possibly be in shooting such birds? Yet one saw this done over and over again, year after year, and in many cases I believe it was due to sheer ignorance. The Badminton Library, the Fur and Feather series, and a host of more modern books all dealing with the same subject, might never have been written. But what astonishes is that frequent experience of the same result did not in itself suggest a remedy, or at any rate the advisability of experimenting. For in those days it was possible to experiment at a low cost. To-day innovations except in a very small way are so costly as to be prohibitive.

It would take too long, and would very likely be profitless as well, to discuss in detail the various methods of making pheasants fly well in flat country—a difficult business it must be admitted. If what has already been said during the last fifty years by the best authorities down to the present day has had so little effect in so many instances, any elaboration of the subject by the author of this book, whether from his own experience, or from the works of others, would be superfluous. All I propose to do here, therefore, is to give the barest indication of the methods which have been tried and found successful. Unless he be an intelligent man, and large-minded as well, the last man to be consulted is the keeper. Keepers as a rule are dreadfully conservative, and prone to regard any change as unnecessary, especially if the proposed arrangement is going to give them extra trouble. My advice would be to talk things over with your keeper if he is the right sort; if not, just tell him what you mean to do, and if he makes difficulties, let him understand that if he declines to meet your views he will have to look out for another place. I am prepared to guarantee that there will be no more trouble.

The writer is well aware, of course, that practically all our large landowners and many others took a pride in showing pheasants as high as they could possibly be made to fly according to the nature of the ground, whether hilly or the reverse, before the war put a stop to pheasant rearing, and reduced many landowners to a state not far removed from penury. Probably pheasant shooting as it flourished in Edwardian days will not be seen in England for many years, if ever again. The breaking up of big estates, combined with depleted incomes have reduced game preservation to a shadow of what it was before 1914. But if a third war is happily averted, we may expect to see a gradual improvement in present-day conditions, and covert-shooting may once again take its place as a regular event in the shooting calendar.

In every method for making pheasants fly, the principle is always the same, namely, to push them on their legs away from the covert where they are accustomed to be fed, and having got them at a sufficient distance to flush them so that they will fly back to it. This is easy if suitable coverts, not too big, are situated a few hundred yards from the main covert. A root field does almost as well. For some reason known best to themselves pheasants always fly well out of root crops. The birds are driven into it on their legs up to a line of stops at the

far end. The guns, meanwhile, will have been placed outside
the wood at such distance from the near end of the root field as
will ensure the birds coming to them at their best pace. The
few men required to flush the pheasants now come forward as
if to drive the reluctant birds out to the stops. Nothing will
make them face the music. Up they get, and with one accord
rise high, and turn back over the beaters, as they make for
home and fancied security. Before reaching it, they catch
sight of the guns and rise still higher, affording as good
shooting as can be desired. In all flushing, whether from roots
or covert, the great thing to guard against is a simultaneous
flush, a manœuvre sometimes practised by an unscrupulous
keeper to allow his birds to escape unshot at. One man alone
advancing in the end may suffice, or at most two or three.
Experiment will soon decide this point, and indeed experiments can be made in a dozen different ways according to the
nature of the flushing point, its distance from the main covert,
and whether situated on rising ground or the reverse. Anyone who has once experienced how pheasants can be made to
fly in the flattest country will never again be a party to the
mowing down of birds, little better in their restricted flight
than farmyard fowls.

There is one exception to the possibility of making pheasants
fly well in flat country, and that is when the only covert is a
large wood of anything from twenty to fifty acres, with no
other cover within a mile of it. Nothing will make pheasants
fly well out of this wood, for the simple reason that they have
nowhere else to go. The only measures that are at all likely to
be of any use are to cut wide rides, encourage thick undergrowth at some distance from the rides as flushing points, and
to divide the wood into portions. Then instead of driving the
pheasants over the guns in the rides, treat each portion as if it

93

were a separate copse, driving the birds on their legs and wings from the part in which they have always been fed into another portion sufficiently distant which must be guarded by a line of stops to prevent them running out. The beaters now come round, and drive the birds back over the line of guns placed several hundred yards behind.

All this involves much labour and expense, and is really not worth while, for the extent of covert is so great that the birds will defeat the best laid plans to marshal and keep them in one portion, while the guns are placed in another to deal with them as they are driven back. Many will escape at the sides, and those that have remained, although they may come over at a fair height are more likely than not also to make for the sides, and so give shots only to one or other of the guns posted on the flanks.

The quickest shooting I ever saw at bad birds, or indeed, at any others, was performed by an American, a guest at a syndicate-shoot in Suffolk, of which I was a member for one wasted season. The guns, posted some thirty yards apart at the edge of a bare field, formed a half-circle round, and within half a dozen yards of, the covert, which here jutted out into a sort of promontory. Adjoining our field were others; some had been ploughed, but all were perfectly bare, with no other cover within a mile of the wood which was being beaten. In fact, the absurd arrangement deprecated in the foregoing pages, and with which I had by now become distressingly familiar, was being carried out with due solemnity. The reluctant birds were pushed out to our very toes, and as they with difficulty rose through the undergrowth they were "downed" one after the other by my American neighbour, as soon as they had risen above the beaters' heads. It was an amazing but a sorry spectacle. The executioner-in-chief, as I may call him, was

94

shooting with a pair of guns and a loader, although Heaven knows, one gun in his hands was more than sufficient. He was, so far as I could see, perfectly safe, but he shot and changed guns like greased lightning, to use an expression of which I am sure he would have approved. He had ten birds down in as many seconds, and the only reason he hadn't fifty was because they weren't there to be shot. What is more, they were all shot in the head or neck, as I happened to know, for I helped to pick some of them up. I don't think any of them had been allowed to get more than fifteen feet from the ground, and one and all were shot at an outside range of ten yards. I personally killed one bird as it was going back over the beaters' heads, and thereafter stood my gun against a tree, and watched the performer on my right. Up would blunder a brace of pheasants with a prodigious clatter. "Crack, crack" would go his gun, and almost before they had reached the ground he had changed guns and was ready for the next. He was certainly "quick on the draw", as he would very likely have termed it. It would have been a real pleasure to see him shoot driven partridges.

Like many Americans, my acquaintance had the charming manners and old-world courtesy which nowadays seems to be more general in the New World than in the Old. I am convinced that he had not the slightest notion that his performance was in any degree unsporting, or that pheasants should be shot in any other way. He probably thought he was taking part in the usual method of covert-shooting as practised in England. He had been asked to shoot pheasants, and if the birds fluttered up almost in his face, that was no fault of his, and the quicker he shot the more he was likely to bag. From a sporting point of view nothing could be more deplorable, but as an exhibition of snap-shooting it was superb.

95

CONTRASTS

O gorgeous bird of brilliant hue,
   When flushed afar how well you flew!
   Your too great pace still greater grew
     As you came nigher,
   And high before, on nearer view
     You seemed still higher.

Whether you crashed from perfect aim,
   Or, missed in style, still onward came,
   And passing left us all to blame
     For aim distorted,
   We ranked you high as sporting game,
     And you we courted.

But when in running from your foes
    You hid in bramble bush, and rose
    Reluctant at our very toes,
        How could we shoot you?
    As soon belabour you with blows
        As thus salute you!

We do adjure you to refrain
    From tempting us with sordid gain,
    But flying high strive to maintain
        Your reputation,
The while you further, free from stain,
        Our education.

CHAPTER XII

WOODCOCK

Habits and Habitat

IN SPITE OF ALL THAT has been written about the woodcock
there is still much that we can only surmise, as must be the
case to some extent with all migratory fowl. But the woodcock
is nocturnal or at any rate crepuscular as well as being migratory, which adds to the difficulty of observation. It seems
doubtful whether woodcock are on the increase in these islands.
As more and more of the larger estates come under the hammer
and are divided up, and as towns encroach more and more on
the country, there must be less inducement than there was for
the woodcock to breed in England. If ever there was a bird
which demands quiet it is the woodcock, and except in a few
favoured localities conditions suited to the birds' requirements
are lacking. The North-Eastern, Eastern and South-Western
seaboards, and the wilder parts of the Welsh coast, are the

98

places most frequented by the woodcock in England and Wales; but the bird wanders inland, taking up its quarters wherever suitable conditions are found, and there is hardly a county in England or Wales that does not produce its small quota of 'cock at every covert shoot. Like the snipe, however, the woodcock is given to shifting its quarters for no apparent reason, and of no bird can it be said with more truth that it is here to-day and gone to-morrow.

But the woodcock's real strongholds in the British Isles are on the west coast of Scotland and Ireland. Game laws have always been ignored in Ireland more or less, and at present there is no sign of any tightening up of legislation against poaching. Consequently the unfortunate woodcock gets scant protection, and the wonder is that it should be as plentiful as it is in Southern Ireland. For this the climate and flora are largely responsible, both suiting the woodcock's requirements to perfection.

Toll in no small numbers is taken of the woodcock in the Scandinavian Peninsula, and in Denmark, where many are shot during the period of migration, and also trapped for sale. This must appreciably affect the number of birds that survive to reach this country. It is a subject of general remark that during the last few years the number of 'cock flushed in the British Isles during the shooting season has shown a marked falling off. On the other hand more are said to breed with us than formerly, but this is a very difficult matter to prove, and statistics in a few favoured localities where woodcock are specially preserved and ringed do not throw much light on the subject as a whole.

From all accounts woodcock used to be much more plentiful in Ireland than they are to-day. Certainly in a game-book kept for generations back in County Clare, where I was one of a party of guns a few years ago, the bag on shooting days even twenty years previously far exceeded our totals. But that autumn there had been disastrous gales, and reports were frequent of drowned woodcock having been found washed up on the Irish coast. But the previous year's totals were equally poor, and so were those of the year before. Again, as bearing on the subject, although it actually proves nothing, the writer recalls many more years ago than he cares to remember, getting excellent woodcock shooting in County Cork near Macroom, on the river Lee. The banks were clothed in holly bushes, and there seemed to be a woodcock, and sometimes two, under every bush. Those were the days! I had an Irish gillie and his dog as my sole attendants. I walked a little ahead on turf as smooth almost as an English lawn, and the gillie whacked the bushes. I didn't get nearly as many 'cock as I ought to have got, but I got more than a few, and I never enjoyed a week's shooting more. I stayed at a dirty little hotel in Macroom, and every morning was driven six miles to the river in a wonderful old gig drawn by a raw-boned Irish mare, which, with her long raking stride, did the journey in half an hour. Arrived at the river, we took boat to the other bank and there the fun began. I am ashamed to say that I have forgotten the gillie's name, for he was a treasure. I gave him 2s. 6d. a day and his lunch with which he was more than content, for I had the greatest difficulty in making him take a small tip at the end. To-day your Irish gillie demands ten shillings a day for lazing in a boat most of the time, plus his lunch and "porther". I speak here of the Irish fishing gillie, but I expect his shooting confrère is by now just as keen on the shekels, at any rate on the beaten track. To do the Southerner justice he is not as a rule naturally greedy, and no one could possibly be keener on sport, but English visitors, with the help of fishing hotels, have made him avaricious.

But to return to the woodcock. Like the snipe it has a very wide range, extending from Siberia in the North to the Azores and Canary Islands in the Atlantic, and from the shores of the Mediterranean to the Himalayas, and, according to Hume, through Mongolia to Japan. That the woodcock breeds in the Himalayas seems certain, since nests with eggs have been found at 10,000 feet, but it is scarce. I once flushed a woodcock in Kashmir at 12,000 feet in October when after barasingh, but do not remember to have seen another in that country. It is perhaps too cold for them, for they are comparatively common at 8,000 feet round Ootacamund, in the Nilgiris, where I have shot several. They would be more common still, were it not for the fact that there is at least one shikari to every woodcock, and one sahib, on leave or retired, to every two of them. So the birds get more than a little harried, and sport suffers from an excess of competition. I have shot an occasional 'cock within a mile or two of Quetta in Baluchistan, but, not surprisingly perhaps, they are few and far between.

Woodcock come to this country from Norway, Denmark, and Holland from the middle of October to the beginning of December, and to the north and west coast of Ireland, via Scotland. The actual time of arrival is, of course, dependent on the weather, but in Ireland at any rate it is not much use looking for 'cock before November. A cold spell in Northern Europe, together with a bright moon and still nights, is favourable to migration, and by the end of November most of the foreigners have arrived. With the exception of those birds which remain to breed in these islands, the returning migration takes place in March or April to the breeding grounds of

Scandinavia and Northern Russia. Sandars says that the females are the first to arrive, presumably in the British Isles, but though respect must be paid to any statement by so great an authority, it is difficult to see how this can be proved, except by the capture of a large number of woodcock on the direct route of migration, and subsequent autopsy. The females are said to be larger than the males. If so, this is the only external difference between the sexes.

The woodcock is not, I think, a difficult bird to shoot in a general way. The bird when flushed in the day-time is generally half asleep. At least it is when put up in an English covert. But have him driven by Irish beaters and he shows his quality. He is terrified by the yells of "hi-cock, hi-cock", by the thrashing of many sticks, and the yapping of the mongrel pack which usually forms part of the beating establishment in Ireland, and dashes through the trees more like forked lightning than the owl-like apparition which so often appears at an English covert-shoot. I never knew how woodcock could fly until I saw them driven in Ireland, and never realised before how very easy it was to miss them. Not that I haven't missed them often enough elsewhere, and sometimes without the shadow of excuse. Two things, I believe, contribute more to the missing of woodcock than of any other game-birds. The first is over-eagerness which tempts sportsmen to loose off at a woodcock at distances at which they would never think of firing at any other bird, and, moreover, to fire hurriedly as well. The other is the deceptive flight. A woodcock even when apparently just flitting through the trees is invariably going much faster than it appears to be. Often, of course, a 'cock offers only a snap shot and a pretty quick one at that, and one must take the chance then or not at all. But when a woodcock offers a fair chance in the open, misses would occur, I believe, less often if one took as much care over one's shot as one would if shooting at a partridge. And I am quite sure that when firing at 'cock it is a sound principle to hold well ahead. Those long sweeping wing-beats are very deceptive.

A most fascinating bird is the woodcock, perhaps of all game-birds the most fascinating. Beautiful in appearance, so rich and delicate in the colouring of the plumage, its ways are as charming as its looks, and that is saying a great deal. To watch woodcock flitting in large circles over woods at dusk in the breeding season, uttering their peculiar twice-repeated croak every few seconds is delightful, particularly if there should be more than one bird in the air at the same time. They seem to love glades, and the bird will cross and recross the same clearing over and over again, but always at the commencement of, or at the completion of, the circular flight. That is to say, that no abrupt turn is made, but the bird having crossed the opening continues on its wide sweep, disappearing from view sometimes for minutes together. Then one hears the now familiar "croak, croak" and looking up sees the 'cock again heading for the glade, though it may be from the opposite direction. I once saw three woodcock "roding" at the same time on the shores of Lough Erne in County Fermanagh, and there may have been more. Only by seeing the birds in the air at the same time could one be certain of the actual number, as they kept disappearing and reappearing at considerable intervals.

I watched this performance for several nights in succession during June, and was struck by the punctuality of the birds' appearance. The flight began about ten o'clock as far as I remember, and was over by twenty minutes past. Sometimes I waited until it was quite dark, but never heard woodcock "roding" after dark, and night after night the flight had stopped while it was still light enough to see the bird against the sky.

Then one night, early in July, the shutters went up. There was no performance either that evening or subsequently. Had the eggs hatched out? Presumably, and probably on this account other 'cock had previously ceased flighting one by one, as family responsibilities claimed their attention. I am sorry now that I did not make a note of the number of woodcock seen "roding" each night, together with the date. There were generally at least two birds flighting at the same time, but occasionally only one; and though it did not occur to me at the time, I think now that the solo performance most probably occurred later in the season, after the others had dropped out.

Talking of the punctuality of woodcock, reminds me that at a camp in the Chin Hills on the Burma-Manipur border, at an elevation of some 8,000 feet, we used to shoot woodcock in October as they flighted from the forest to their feeding grounds at dusk, incidentally furnishing proof of the bird's extensive range. There was a small rest-house at this camp which was known by the name of Bamboo Camp, from the bamboo forest in which the bungalow was situated. A ravine ran up to the front of the rest-house forming a short opening in the forest, and up this ravine the woodcock invariably flighted, making straight for the rest-house over which they passed, not to reappear presumably until dawn. Two or three of us would be seated in long cane chairs on the grass plot in front of the rest-house, with our legs comfortably cocked up on the extended sides, a cigarette between our lips, and a drink handy at our elbow, when someone would look at his watch and say "woodcock time", an announcement bringing us instantly to our feet. Glasses would be hurriedly drained, cigarettes flung on the grass, and picking up our guns we would advance a few paces to the head of the ravine, there to await the arrival of *Scolopax rusticola*, to give him his not unpleasing scientific designation. Nor had we long to wait. Almost to the minute a wavering form would appear flying straight up the ravine, for all the world like a large bat, the long bill clearly silhouetted against the darkening sky. Usually a volley would greet its approach, and more often than not the bird, with the same apparently laboured flight, would pass over our heads unscathed, to vanish into the gloom beyond the rest-house. It would be followed by another and yet another, at almost regular intervals of two or three minutes until six or seven woodcock in all had run the gauntlet. The most I ever saw brought down were two. The next evening at precisely the same time the scene would be repeated and, in spite of the preceding night's fusillade which one might suppose would have scared the birds out of their senses, the same flickering bat-like creature would appear in the same place, in the same direction, and at the same unhurried pace. Nor do I recollect any decrease in numbers—there were always five or six woodcock to brave our very indifferent musketry. Personally I never hit one I am glad to say, for it seems rather a mean trick not far removed from poaching, to take advantage of the weakness of so sporting a bird, if one can call what appears to be an overpowering instinct a weakness. Not that I did not do my best, but those were the days in which my gun and I were invariably at loggerheads.

In extenuation of our misdeeds I have, I maintain, three very good excuses to offer. The first, that owing to the call of duty our stay at this camp was confined to two or three days at most. It became, therefore, a matter of making the most of limited opportunities. The second, that in such an out-of-the-way spot inhabited only by a jungle tribe, and visited by white officials once in a blue moon, we were doing no harm to anybody by shooting a few woodcock in the open season, and precious little harm as it happened to the woodcock themselves. Moreover, owing to the denseness and extent of the jungle, if one didn't shoot woodcock there when flighting, one would never shoot, or indeed see, them at all. And the third, and possibly most convincing excuse of all, that having existed for months on tinned food eked out by the tough and stringy fowl of the East, misnamed a chicken, a *bonne bouche* in the shape of a woodcock on toast was not to be lightly disregarded.

A woodcock's nest is by no means easy to find, so cunningly does the bird hide her treasures in the fallen leaves and bracken which exactly tone with the coloration of the eggs, and with that of the bird itself. It is now a well-established fact that the woodcock carries her young to the feeding ground, and also removes them to a safer spot when danger threatens. The reason that this unique sight has been witnessed by comparatively few individuals is due to the bird's nocturnal habits. The flight to the feeding ground is only made at dusk, and the return at the earliest sign of dawn. In a darkening light the bird itself would be almost invisible unless silhouetted against the sky, and maternal instinct as well as her burden would induce the woodcock when carrying her young to fly low between the trees rather than above them. In such conditions even if the bird itself is seen, it would, except in very favourable circumstances, be almost impossible to be sure that it was carrying anything. From all accounts it has been chiefly in the day-time that the woodcock has been seen to carry its young, doubtless with a view to removing them from a dangerous situation to a place of safety.

A FAMILY PICTURE

Safe in her plumage of warm golden brown,
Toning with bracken and with fallen leaves,
Snug in the ferns that match her russet gown,
The nesting 'cock the keenest eye deceives;
The while her mate at dawn and eventide
Flies croaking round puffed out with love-sick pride.

"Roding" 'tis called, a fascinating sight,
Enjoyed each evening when the bright lights fade;
At times more 'cock join in the nuptial flight,
Disporting in this elfish serenade;
Like monstrous bats flitting when sun has set,
Long bill and body clear in silhouette.

And when four downy chicks complete her brood,
And from maternal care begin to stray,
How shall I paint the dam's solicitude
When danger threatens? How her wiles portray?
As with disabled wing and lagging pace
She lures some clumsy human from the place.

Nay more, when fresh disturbance peace outlaws,
Or flight to distant feeding grounds is made,
She picks her young up neatly in her claws,
And bears them one by one to some safe glade;
With chick to body firmly clasped she flies,
And till they're safe all food for self denies.

Assembled at some marshy ooze, what joy
Is theirs throughout a warm and starlit night!
With nothing now to hinder or annoy,
And food in plenty for their heart's delight.
What stampings, and what probings in the soil
To circumvent the fat and wriggling spoil!

And when the mother has withdrawn a worm,
How quick the youngsters run to get their share!
Tug-tugging at the red and writhing form
Until they rend and gulp the luscious fare;
And if for further details I am pressed
Imagination must supply the rest.

Here we may leave the family complete,
The downy youngsters growing day by day,
Sleeping their meal off in the noonday heat
In sheltering bush of holly or of bay.
And let us hope Dame Fortune (within reason)
Will keep them safe throughout the shooting season.

CHAPTER XIII

WOODCOCK SHOOTING

On three occasions I have had the chance of a "right and left" at woodcock, but I have never brought it off, although I was once lucky enough to bag a snipe and a woodcock with a "right and left", an unusual combination. This happened a few years ago in Essex outside a wood which generally held a 'cock or two. I had drawn a blank in the wood, so walked up a marshy piece of meadow adjoining the covert, on the off chance of a snipe. I had almost come to the end when I flushed a snipe which fell to the right barrel. At the report a 'cock, greatly to my astonishment, rose almost at my feet, and I got him just in time with the left barrel as he dived over a hedge. I think it must have flitted out of the wood unseen on hearing me coming through, and have settled in the marsh.

On two of the three occasions above mentioned, I got one bird instead of a couple, once by having to fire two barrels at the same bird, and the other time through no fault of mine. The keeper with the help of a brace of spaniels put up two 'cock out of a brambly dell. One gave a difficult chance as it

109

jinked low through the trees, but luck was on my side and I knocked it over. The other made one of its abrupt turns towards me, and then flew steadily away against a saffron-tinted sky, the effect of a glorious sunset. It was a chance in a thousand, and I would have betted 100 to 1 against the bird. But a woodcock is an unpredictable creature, and I would have lost my bet, for as I pressed the trigger it dived suddenly downwards, and was instantly lost to sight against a background of dark firs, and that was that. My shot could not have been within a yard of it, and so I lost my third and last chance of a "right and left" at woodcock, for I have never had another.

But my first chance remains to be described, although I am almost ashamed to relate it. It happened just thirty years ago, but the scene and the incidents are as clear in my memory as if it had only occurred yesterday. Three of us were shooting rabbits on a steep and gorse-clad hillside in Banffshire. It was an early and hard winter, and although only the first week in December, snow lay thick on the ground, entirely covering the smaller clumps of gorse. The fun was fast and furious. We had between us four hard-bitten spaniels, and every piece of gorse seemed to hold a rabbit. My post was at the top of the slope, while the other two guns worked up from below. We were all kept busy, and what with a constant fusillade, encouragement of the dogs, shouts of warning to each other, and the yapping of the spaniels the din was terrific. We had shot a dozen rabbits in half as many minutes, and the sport was beginning to wane. I had just shot a rabbit, when I noticed a slight quiver of a small gorse-bush not more than a foot high, and, except for a few spikes, entirely covered with snow. This little bush was only a yard or so from me, so having reloaded I took a pace forward to stir up the reluctant bunny. My surprise may be imagined when instead of the expected rabbit, up got a couple of woodcock, which through all the din and commotion had been sheltering in the sparse cover afforded by this tiny bush. They flew off at no great pace showing well against the sky, one at right-angles to the other, and I fired at each in turn and missed them both! To this day I cannot think what happened, and can only suppose that I was so taken aback by the unexpected apparition that I fired hurriedly, without the slightest need for hurry. We were all stricken with silence as we watched the departing woodcock. Then one of the party murmured "Bad luck!" or something equally decent if untrue, and for some time afterwards conversation languished. For myself, the fact that I remember it so vividly after all these years, is proof how deeply the iron penetrated my soul. Of all my misses this was surely the most distressing, for the double chance was such a "sitter", and the prize so eminently desirable.

But when I conjure up the vision of these two innocents sitting huddled up together in their most inadequate shelter, half-petrified with cold and fright in the midst of a devastating din, I could almost persuade myself that I am glad to have missed them, and of course, if such a chance ever occurred again. . . .

WOODCOCK FINESSE

You may speak with shame of the three card game,
  And your efforts to spot the "Lady",
But I know a trick that's twice as slick,
  With an end that's just as shady,
Played by a sprite with an owl's slow flight,
  And a mug's long-pointed bill,
As black as jet in silhouette
  Between the sky and hill;
Flying high in a saffron sky,
  A positive gift for the gun,
And you thank the gods, and you'd lay the odds
  At a confident ten to one:
But you'd lose your bet, for your silhouette
  —I'll swear I heard it snigger—
Has dived in a curve with a lightning swerve
  As your finger pressed the trigger,
And the gorse and the bracken have swallowed it up,
And the gods of the mountain have "sold you a pup".

Well, here's to our "owl" as it sails away,
And we'll talk about mugs another day!

SNIPE APPROACHING EGGS

A FALLING PIGEON

CHAPTER XIV

SNIPE

As of the woodcock, so much has been written of the snipe that little now remains to be said on the subject. One can but touch on one's own reactions to the bird's idiosyncrasies, giving the reason for any personal predilection in the matter of its pursuit.

The snipe follows the same migration routes to these islands as the woodcock, and has, if anything, an even more extended range. From Siberia in the North throughout Europe to Natal in South Africa, and possibly even farther south, and through Arabia, Persia, India and China in the East, the common or full snipe is found wherever bog, marsh, or rice fields (in the east) produce the supply of worms which form its staple diet, and without which it cannot long exist. In India the snipe occurs in extraordinary numbers in suitable localities, and is also plentiful in Burma and China. In Africa, Morocco and Egypt are its principal strongholds. In America it is replaced by an allied species, the Wilson snipe, and in Southern India and the Malay States by the Pintail snipe (*Gallinago stenura*).

8

Of the three species of snipe which migrate to these islands the common snipe is by far the most plentiful, hence its name. It is also the only snipe that breeds here. The other two are the jack snipe and the great snipe (*Gallinago media*). The last is so rare as to be seldom met with. Since any rare game-bird is a prize, it is somewhat surprising that the great snipe has often been mistaken for an extra-large specimen of the common snipe, although its distinguishing characteristics are easily memorised. These are, firstly, its sluggish straightforward flight, secondly, the belly is spotted instead of white as in the common snipe, and thirdly, the great snipe has sixteen feathers in its tail against the fourteen tail feathers of the common snipe, and the two outer tail feathers are pure white.

The jack snipe while nowhere plentiful in these islands is by no means rare. It seems to be even more particular than the common snipe as to feeding grounds. Some bogs always hold a few jack; in others they are never seen. I have noticed that it is generally found on soft quaky ground, and is often missed on this account. Just as you are negotiating a particularly nasty bit—one of those treacherous pieces of vivid green—up springs a jack under your feet, and as likely as not escapes the shaky aim natural to a man anchored firmly by both legs in the slimy morass that threatens to engulf him. But if its destruction is sought, poor Jack soon comes to an untimely end, for so confiding is the little bird that it settles again within a hundred yards or so, and if it can be induced to rise again—by no means a certainty—it is not likely to be missed a second time, as it flits away in its curious butterfly flight. When common snipe are at all plentiful jack are often spared, for such diminutive morsels, weighing but two ounces, are hardly worth powder and shot. But they are well worth shooting in a hard frost, for when the common snipe has hardly any flesh on its bones, its small congener will be as fat as butter. It is able to pick up a living when the common snipe would starve.

Sometimes jack are found in numbers in certain localities. When this occurs I believe it to be due to a recent arrival of migrants. I had an experience of this once in Egypt during the first world war. We were stationed at Ismailia on the Suez Canal, and under the guidance of a fellaheen who acted as shikari, a brother officer and I took train to a station a few miles up the line on the little single-line railway that used to run between Suez and Port Said, and probably still does. From there a short trek took us to a small marsh, which was simply alive with jack snipe. At every step a jack would spring up and flit away. It was a startling sight. The shikari thought so too, for as each bird rose he greeted it with a loud "hoo" of astonishment, while his arm went up for all the world like a semaphore. After we had severally missed half a dozen birds, I turned on our attendant in a spasm of irritation born of our misses, and consigned him to a place also beginning with an h to match his "hoo". Reprehensible, no doubt, but effective, for it reduced him to silence, and the semaphore to inaction. The change was immediate, for at once we began to hit them, and in a short time had collected some twenty couple of jack, as memory serves, on a marsh barely an acre in extent, and on which there was not a single common snipe. From there we went to another and larger marsh, a mile or so distant, and this was full of the common snipe, and if there were any jack at all, they were so few that I have no recollection of seeing them. I have forgotten what our bag was, but I know it was satisfactory. Much to our regret we were unable to make another trip of the same kind, as the regiment was shortly ordered elsewhere, and I have never had another opportunity of shooting snipe in

Egypt. The month was November, and I think we must have struck a "fall" of jack probably only a day or two before our visit. But it was curious that there should not have been a single full snipe in that very attractive little marsh, or, conversely, that there should have been no jack snipe or none worth mentioning, in the larger marsh only a mile or two away.

The jack is the handsomest of all the snipes. The back is a metallic olive green and brown with a beautiful sheen on the feathers. As one picks up a jack one is struck at once by the gamey appearance of the little bird. Unlike the common snipe it rises quite silently, that is, it utters no vocal sound, but there is often a distinct flutter as it springs up.

All shooting men know of, if they have not actually witnessed, the drumming of the common snipe during the breeding season. For a long time controversy raged as to whether the curious sound like the bleating of a goat was made vocally, or whether it was produced by the wings, or tail feathers, or by both. Even now the matter is not entirely decided. Nearly all are agreed that the sound is not vocal, but some think that the half-closed wings set up vibration against the tail feathers, and so cause the drumming, while others, and perhaps the majority, are of opinion that the two outer tail feathers, standing as they do at right-angles to the bird's body when it stoops or planes, alone produce the drumming, by the vibration of the air against them in the snipe's downward swoop. That the sound was produced from the bird's throat was easily disproved from the fact that the snipe sometimes utters a twice-repeated note when courting, which has been described as "tchik-tchak, tchik-tchak", and has been heard to utter this call while actually drumming.

The drumming of the snipe can be heard wherever the bird

breeds from March to June, generally from dawn to an hour or two later and again in the evening till dark. I have heard snipe drumming long after dusk, when trees were only visible against the skyline, and when it was much too dark to see the birds themselves; and they are said to drum at intervals throughout moonlight nights. How strange that aerial forms of courtship should be confined to the *Scolopax* family, and to no other birds so far as we know! No bird but the woodcock rodes, and no bird drums but the snipe. Other birds go through aerial evolutions in the spring, pigeons and peewits for example, but none in the remarkable and systematic manner of the snipe and woodcock. Both of these in common with many other birds display on the ground before the lady of their choice, in addition to their aerial performances, puffing themselves out, and strutting with drooping wings. The woodcock at any rate has been seen to display in this manner, but the evidence as regards the snipe rests, so far as I can gather, on the behaviour of a tame snipe belonging to Mr. Hugh Wormald as quoted in *British Birds* (*Magazine*) II 249 "In the spring his bird was said to make a kind of display by walking round and round his hand and uttering the spring note, while spreading the tail fanwise and gently poking his hand with his beak."[1]

Like the woodcock, the snipe lays four eggs pyriform in shape, and very large for the size of the bird, with dark-brown blotches on a greenish background, but the colouring is very variable. The nest itself is a depression in heather, rushes, or in a tussock of grass, in a marshy spot, and is formed by intertwined grasses. It is carefully concealed, and like the woodcock's, difficult to find, unless the bird is accidentally flushed when sitting.

[1] *British Sporting Birds*, p. 159.

Snipe Shooting

No bird has aroused more controversy than the snipe. Whether to walk down-wind on a snipe, or up-wind, or across; whether to take it the instant it rises, or to wait until it has finished twisting, has been the subject of debate in print, and whenever sportsmen foregather, ever since shooting at birds flying was first practised, and doubtless will continue to be debated as long as there are snipe to shoot and sportsmen to shoot them. But as Sir Ralph Payne-Gallwey says, "Our little friend flies through all laws and advice with room and to spare."[1]

The very fact that there has been, and still is, so much controversy on the subject is in itself a tribute to the fascination of snipe-shooting. For fascinating it is, holding its votaries in bonds until old-age or illness debars them from further pursuit. Not to be out of fashion, let us join in the debate as to the best methods of shooting snipe. I purposely avoid using the word controversy, for all disputation or laying down the law is to be avoided. I can but state the methods which suit myself best, giving the pros and cons and leaving others to follow or avoid them as they please.

First, then, I would mention a condition which is even more important than the wind, but which, curiously enough, I never remember hearing discussed, or to have seen mentioned in print. I refer to the light, and this particularly affects the shooter in glasses. It is worth while making a big detour to get the sun at your back, whatever the direction of the wind, and this whether the sun is shining in a cloudless sky, or obscured by clouds. Wherever the sun is, there will be glare, and a snipe flying into even a subdued glare is an indistinct wraith, which, after the manner of wraiths, is utterly impervious to shot, or

[1] *Shooting: Moor and Marsh* (The Badminton Library), p. 144.

perhaps I should say my shot, for you may be able to hit such a snipe; I cannot. Then background is often worth considering. Where conditions of light are equal, as when the sun is on one's flank, it is well to arrange, if possible, to advance on the snipe from a direction that will give a shot against the sky, rather than against, say, a wood, or a spinney of fir-trees, or a hill—anything in fact that will tone with the protective colouring of the snipe, and "lose him on you" as they say in Ireland. He will be "lost on you" often enough in spite of all precautions, but a little trouble may make all the difference between failure and success.

As to the wind, I am personally indifferent whether I walk down or across the wind. But I always feel unhappy if I have to walk up-wind on snipe. The snipe's hearing is extremely keen, and I do not think it makes a particle of difference in this respect whether the advance is made up-wind or down. The birds hears one just the same. My experience of walking up-wind is that the snipe skims away close to the ground jinking like a thing possessed, particularly if the wind be strong, as only by keeping low can it progress against it. When walking down-wind on snipe in a stiff breeze, often enough the bird as it rises seems to be swept away, and is out of shot almost before the gun can be raised to the shoulder; but if lying fairly well, snipe rising against the wind (as they must) frequently hang in the air for the nth of a second, just giving time for a quick shot before they turn with the wind, and cross, as they often do, to right or left of the shooter. It is impossible, of course, to walk down- or across-wind all the time, but when in traversing a big bog or marsh I am obliged on turning to take an up-wind beat, I know that I shall miss every snipe, and sure enough I do. Another advantage of walking down-wind on snipe is that as the bird turns, it often presents its white breast for an instant to the shooter, and such a chance is not to be despised, especially if against a dark background.

I have said that in my opinion snipe can hear equally well for all practical purposes whether one walks down- or up-wind. And the more I see of snipe the more convinced I am that this is so. Considerations affecting the wildness of snipe or the reverse will be discussed later, but it may be said briefly here that if snipe are lying well they are not a bit more likely to rise "wild" if approached down-wind than up. Conversely, if they are wild they will be so however approached. Snipe at best are shy and wary birds, but if they have fed well overnight, and it is not too windy, they will lie fairly well, if they have not been recently disturbed, and if the approach is made quietly. I use the expression "fairly well" advisedly, for in these islands one does not expect snipe to lie as they do in the East under the influence of a hot sun, unlimited feeding, and a warm temperature of the water.

As to the actual shot at snipe, I have tried waiting for the jinking to subside and have almost invariably waited in vain. Now and again one may anticipate the twist, but whenever this occurs I always feel that I have fluked a lucky shot. Speaking for myself, I find the surest way is to take a snipe the moment it rises, or as soon after as may be, covering the bird as the trigger is pressed. By this method there is often time for a second shot, if a miss is scored by the first barrel; also one has a chance of a "right and left" if two snipe have risen at the same time. Hanging on to one's aim, I find, is fatal. So rapid is the twisting, and so erratic, that it is impossible to foresee where the bird will be when the shot arrives. If the twists were made at regular intervals, however short, it would be comparatively an easy matter to anticipate them. But you cannot with any certainty anticipate the movements of a creature which is giving a lively imitation of forked lightning. The best chance afforded at a going-away snipe is, I believe, at the moment when it springs from the ground, before it has time to start its evolutions. Certainly the best shot I ever saw in India on snipe dealt with them in this manner. No sooner was the bird up than it was down, for he seldom missed, but for quickness combined with accuracy he was unsurpassed. True, the snipe in India lies better and twists less than the snipe at home, but the principle is the same, and I have not the slightest doubt that when the sportsman referred to shot snipe in the British Isles, he took them precisely in the same way as he did in India.

The only advantage I can see in waiting is that when a snipe rises fairly close, by the time it has reached a distance of forty to forty-five yards it may possibly be clearly outlined against the sky, but it is probably still twisting, so this advantage is neutralised, and the shot pattern at forty-five yards, even with No. 8 is a very open one. On the other hand, if one takes a near bird as it rises or soon after, there is still time for a second shot before it is out of range.

But although I believe in quick shooting at snipe, I do not mean hurried shooting, which is absolutely fatal. (The following is for novices only, please.) Steadiness is essential, and it is quite easy to be quick and steady at the same time. Snipe-shooting tries one's nerves more than any other kind of shooting I know, but until one has acquired rigid self-control good work on snipe cannot be expected. The very rise of a snipe is startling in its unexpectedness, but one must not allow oneself to be startled. At first one cannot help it. Up jumps a snipe, and with it up jumps the gun to the shoulder, and is banged off with practically no sense of direction except that it was pointed somewhere in the neighbourhood of the bird, which is now screeching its way to safety. And the shooter couldn't tell you whether he was above it or below, or to right or left. Should a lark rise, up jumps the gun again and is shamefacedly and quickly lowered. This sort of thing is useless. The shooter should school himself not to raise his gun until he is certain that the rising bird is a snipe, and if it is, not to raise it until he is certain of the direction in which it is heading. Never mind if he is slow at first. Quickness will come before very long. If one or the other must be sacrificed, let it be quickness a hundred times before steadiness. As the gun comes to the shoulder it must be fired at once, or the novice will get into the bad habit of dwelling on his aim, "poking" in fact. Let the gun be brought deliberately up and the trigger pressed as the stock comes home to the shoulder. Afterwards when steadiness is assured the shooter can evolve the method of shooting snipe which he finds best. But steadiness is a *sine qua non*.

I find it pays in snipe shooting to expect rises at twenty-five yards, and to keep one's eyes—when they can be spared from glances at treacherous or difficult footing—steadfastly fixed at this distance ahead. Then if a snipe rises closer than expected, it is so much the easier to deal with. If, on the contrary, one is careless, and looks only ten or fifteen yards ahead, one is much disconcerted when a snipe springs up at some twenty-five yards distance. It is the unexpected that confuses, and if a snipe rises "wild" at the distance one is expecting it, the chances of hitting it are very much more in one's favour than would otherwise be the case. Everyone must have noticed how much easier it is to deal with a snipe to which a dog is standing. True, it sits tighter, but the main reason is that it is *expected* to rise there or thereabouts. Similarly, if one stands still, and gets an attendant to throw a stone or a sod of peat into a likely spot, it is ten to one that if a snipe does rise, it rises only to fall. Once more it is the expected that counts.

The sound a snipe utters on or after rising is generally described as "scape scape". It is a most difficult sound to imitate or to reduce to writing. There is certainly something sibilant about it, but also something harsh and rasping—a screech rather than a note. "Scape" is much too melodious a sound, and really not like it, except in so far as the letters "sc" convey the sibilant sound. "Scarp", which I have seen given as a substitute for "scape", is much nearer the note, but does not represent the staccato screech of the full snipe. It is impossible for the human voice to reproduce the sound, and almost as difficult to convey it in writing, so I must needs be content to leave the matter where it is.

There is one thing about the note, or rather its utterance, that is worthy of notice, since it affects the shooter's chances. Contrary to the general idea, snipe very often rise silently, and only utter the double screech after they have flown some distance, and occasionally not at all, or at any rate not until they have passed out of earshot. It is a help, I think, when a snipe screeches as it rises, because it enables the shooter to concentrate on the bird, if, that is, it doesn't unnerve him! Too often one sees a bird a second too late, when it has risen silently on the flank and slightly behind one. By the time it has screeched it is virtually out of shot. Here again it is the expected that tells. If one expects snipe to rise silently vigilance is increased, and the "scarp, scarp" of the flushed snipe, so far from startling, will be welcome, since it assists concentration.

I have noticed that the closer snipe sit the more likely they are to screech when flushed. This is natural, since the screech is a note of alarm, much as a blackbird shrieks when startled in a hedge. When snipe lie well, it is generally because the bird has fed well during the previous night, and also because the weather is mild for the time of year. It is, therefore, lethargic, and the near approach of a human being startles it, and the screech is the result. On the other hand, when snipe rise wild they are very much on the alert, and are not startled as they would be at the close approach of the common enemy. This perhaps explains why, to the best of my recollection, snipe in India almost invariably rise with a screech. At any rate I never remember noticing the contrary, and considering how abundant snipe are in that country compared with the British Isles, the deferred utterance, if common, could hardly have escaped notice.

SNIPE ELUSIVE

As from your oozy bed you rise
   With startling scurry,
The 12-bore to my shoulder flies
   In frantic hurry.
Where is my calm, my purpose wise
   To banish flurry?

From far you mock the aim untrue
   With screech derisive;
How profitless to mimic you
   With speech incisive!
Much wiser to evolve anew
   A scheme decisive.

I think myself 'tis wrong to wait
   Till twists are over;
The chances are he'll not fly straight
   (The artful mover!)
Until too far for dreaded fate
   To harm our rover.

For near or far, the least delay
   May spell disaster:
Try "poking" and your snipe's away
   And flying faster;
And all you've done by your display
   Is space to plaster!

But near or far, a steady shot
   With speedy aiming
Will do the trick as like as not,
   And do your game in;
And if you miss, at least you've got
   No cause for blaming.

That's my belief, but you may vow
    'Tis a delusion;
That downright methods counselled now
    Tend to confusion;
There's no gainsaying anyhow
    This safe conclusion.

That howsoe'er aim be directed,
Our snipe will do the unexpected!

CHAPTER XV

SNIPE GROUND

MANY MORE SNIPE are found on wet bogs than on any other ground, but this does not always mean that many more will be bagged. Hundreds may be seen, but they may be so wild as to be unapproachable. Splashing, of course, is fatal to success in snipe shooting, and every advantage should be taken of banks and ridges. In a very wet bog for this reason a dog at large does more harm than good, and if one is taken its right place is at heel, or led by an attendant. On a dangerous marsh a shooter should always have someone with him, as at any moment he may be badly bogged.

A day on the mountain with a good ranging setter or pointer is very enjoyable, especially if there should be a fair number of grouse. But one must be a good walker, and be prepared to get wet. The heather itself, often knee-deep, is generally wet from October onwards, and there are treacherous spots at the base of tussocks and elsewhere, hidden by long grass on which it is very easy to place an unwary foot. There is pretty sure to be a fair number of snipe, but widely distributed over a large

127

extent of mountain. Most dogs stand well to snipe, the scent of which seems to possess a special fascination for them. The shots will in consequence, be near ones, but not always easy on that account, for if flushed against the wind the snipe will just skim the heather with which they tone only too well, twisting abominably the while.

But now that I am no longer young and active, and, more-over, having been spoiled by super-excellent snipe-shooting in India, what appeals to me to-day is not a trudge over bog or mountain, but to potter round rushy bottoms with a retriever at heel, in search of the occasional snipe, and mighty content, as friend Pepys would say, if it turns out to be more than merely occasional. Frequently one is unrewarded, but this is more than compensated for by a good morning, when perhaps one fires a dozen shots, and returns with two or three couple of snipe to show for them. The bag is necessarily small, for the ground is limited in extent but there is always pleasureable anticipation, often realised, when one looks up favourite spots in turn in the hope of finding them occupied. This it is, I think, that constitutes the charm of a walk over snipe-haunted meadows, this, and also the satisfaction of manœuvring for position, as it were, so that when a snipe is flushed it may offer the most likely chance to the shooter.

With regard to conditions of weather affecting the wild-ness or the reverse of snipe, I do not think that anything on this subject can be better said than it has been by Sir Ralph Payne-Gallwey when writing on snipe in the Badminton Library Series.[1] "There is no doubt", he says, "that snipe dislike rain, frost and strong winds, and that they lie best in *heavy warm weather*, with a slight breeze and a falling barometer, the latter state of things in winter indicating an approaching storm. The

[1] *Shooting: Moor and Marsh.*

A QUICK CHANGE OVER

COUNTING THE DAY'S BAG

birds being admirable weather prophets have then fed well in prospect of disturbance, and are heavy and sluggish. On bright frosty days especially during white frosts, snipe are certainly fidgety; they then look almost as big and dark as do 'cocks on the wing, and are easier marks than usual, especially if snow covers the ground. In a hard black frost they fly like arrows, and dart away in a moment." (The italics are mine.)

Quiet moonlight or starlight nights are always favourable for snipe shooting on the following day, provided that there has been little or no frost. The snipe will have fed sufficiently to be lethargic when found, or as lethargic as they ever are in this country, and to lie well. Dark or windy nights, or nights of hard frost, mean that the birds have not been able to get a sufficient supply of worms, and that in consequence they will be wild and restless the following day.

It is commonly said in Ireland that when there is a bright moon snipe forsake the meadows, and are only to be found on the "red" bogs. I think there is something in this, although I have never heard a reason given for the statement. I think also that a great deal depends on the type of meadow. The snipe, having fed well, naturally seek seclusion where they can rest in peace until evening draws them to their feeding grounds again. A good many fly to higher ground on the mountain, and there are always snipe on the bogs; but in spite of the above dictum I have often found a fair smattering of snipe in unfrequented rushy meadows after a bright moonlight night, often on the higher ground where it is comparatively dry. There is generally, if not always, a scarcity of snipe on low-lying grassy meadows at the time of full moon, but I believe that this is simply due to the fact that such ground affords inadequate cover, and that those snipe that have fed there during the night betake themselves at dawn or shortly afterwards to more

9

congenial resting places. And the reason that snipe are found on water-meadows and other ground with scanty cover following moonless and dark nights is, I believe, simply because the birds have not been able to get sufficient food during the night, and in consequence are reluctant to leave their feeding grounds until driven from them. So it comes about that some sportsman finding a scarcity of snipe on such ground at the time of a full moon makes the assertion, quite justifiably, that the snipe have gone elsewhere, and so the saying gains ground without the reason being understood. That, at least, is my own interpretation of it.

Mr. De Visme Shaw, writing on snipe in the Fin, Fur and Feather Series,[1] advises the keen snipe-shot to be out at dawn, giving as his reason that within an hour or two of daylight snipe leave their feeding grounds and scatter themselves over the higher country, returning again an hour or two before dark. No doubt he is correct, but if one lives several miles from the nearest snipe ground, as I do, it means rising on a cold winter's morning at the unholy hour of 6 a.m. or thereabouts, getting the car out, and driving off in the dark, to find quite possibly that there are no snipe on the meadows, those uncertain birds having selected this particular night for a raid on adjacent bogs. Or they may be on the meadows, but so wild as to be unapproachable. In India, at any rate, it is hopeless to attempt to shoot snipe before 9 o'clock in the morning. The birds are there all right, but wild as hawks. And the early morning on the plains of India in the cold weather is balmy compared with what it is in the British Isles at the corresponding time of year. However, I am always telling myself that some morning I really must put matters to the proof, but somehow when the morning arrives, or rather is on its way, all I do is to pull the

[1] *Snipe and Woodcock* (Fin, Fur and Feather Series).

blankets tighter round me and go to sleep again. But I have much pleasure in passing on Mr. Shaw's advice to the younger generation in the hope that they, while "idle slumber scorning", may find the added zest to their sport that, to quote Mr. Shaw, "a little personal inconvenience" provides.

From my limited observation I do not think that snipe return to their feeding grounds much before dark. There is no doubt that at dawn, and just before nightfall more snipe will be found than at any other time (since we cannot shoot at night). But early rising for snipe alone would only be worth while if they were both plentiful and lying well, by no means a certainty. And endeavouring to shoot low-flying and twisting snipe in the waning light of a winter's evening is not an amusement which appeals to everybody. For my part, I am content to seek my snipe between 9.30 in the morning and 3 or 4 in the afternoon according to the time of year. Still, some morning, perhaps, when I am feeling more than usually energetic . . .

As to the most suitable gun for snipe, any ordinary game gun should do, unless snipe predominate above all other game. In that case the gun should, I suggest, be a well-balanced 12-bore weighing 6 to 6½ lb., and bored to give improved cylinder results from the right barrel (say, a well-distributed pattern of 140 or thereabouts in the 30-in. circle at 40 yards with No. 6 shot), and full-choke in the left barrel. The full-choke will be found very useful for snipe rising wild, or for a quick second barrel after a miss from the first.

As regards the charge, No. 8 is the ideal size of shot for snipe. Imperial Chemical Industries Ltd. have, or had before the war, a most excellent snipe cartridge, the "Alphamax", loaded with 1¼ oz. of No. 8 shot and Neoflak powder. The big charge of shot is particularly useful on snipe, for which bird pattern is so much more essential than penetration. The recoil is not noticeable unless many shots are fired in rapid succession, or unless the gun is very light. A rubber recoil-pad is a great help in neutralising the effect of recoil. Not long ago using this cartridge and shooting in gloves I pulled the right trigger on a snipe, and inadvertently fired the left barrel at the same time. Wonderful to relate I killed the snipe without blowing it to bits, but the recoil from the double discharge, while distinctly felt, occasioned no unpleasant effects such as a bruised cheek or finger. I feel sure that I owe many a snipe to the "Alphamax" cartridge, which would have escaped at 45 yards the usual charge of $1\frac{1}{16}$ oz. of shot. It is to be hoped that the I.C.I. will again be able to supply this load, not only for snipe-shooting, but for duck and wood pigeon, with the appropriate size of shot.

A word must be said on the vexed question of foot-gear. One can either go out snipe shooting prepared to get wet, or hope to keep dry during the day. The first alternative is, of course, the simplest, and all that is needed is a pair of stout ankle-boots with a thick stocking on the leg and preferably breeches above that, instead of plus-fours which hold the wet about the knees. A change of clothing is of course necessary the moment shooting is over.

I have solved, to my own satisfaction at least, the problem of keeping dry while snipe-shooting, by having light rubber continuations permanently attached to my cording (Newmarket) knee-boots. These extensions reach to the hip, and are so light as to be no impediment in walking, and I find that they wear uncommonly well. By the end of a day's snipe shooting the extensions are generally wet half-way up the thigh, and sometimes I have only just managed to avoid going in over the tops. Once or twice I have failed to avoid this catastrophe. On one occasion I sat down hurriedly in an unexpectedly soft spot, when the continuations were naturally of no avail, but ordinarily they allow of my adventuring with confidence where, in the days of the useful but inadequate gum-boot, I went in fear and trembling. I present the idea to such of my snipe-shooting readers who have passed the hey-day of reckless youth, and who, finding the rubber thigh-boot too heavy, as indeed it is, are still looking for satisfactory gear which will keep them warm and dry with ordinary precaution.

In return, I should be truly grateful for a recommendation of a really suitable glove for shooting. The best thing I know, and it is a poor sort of makeshift, is the woollen glove with a slit for the trigger-finger. But it is useless in rain, and almost as much so in hard weather. Mittens worn underneath help, but it is the extremities that get so cold, and more than once I have missed birds because my finger was too cold to feel the trigger. A stout leather glove lined with lambswool and having only the front part of the trigger-finger made of the finest doeskin might be a possible solution, but such a glove could only be used with a single-trigger gun, and even if the back of the forefinger were protected by wool and leather, it is doubtful whether this would keep the front part from freezing in its thin doeskin covering. Possibly some clever chemist of the future may evolve a solution for painting the fingers to keep them warm, but until then we shooters on the fens and marshes must, I suppose, put up with cold hands, and make the best of it.

A hard frost continued for several days puts an end to snipe-shooting. The birds cannot get the worms on which they depend, and consequently migrate to the south-west coast of Ireland from Scotland and Northern Ireland, and probably also to the south-west coast of England and the

Scilly Isles, some possibly even crossing the Mediterranean into Africa for an adequate food supply—such at least as have the strength to fly so far. It is pitiful to see full snipe in a prolonged frost hardly able to fly, taking shorter flights than jack snipe, and literally having to be poked up; while woodcock are often so weakened by starvation and cold that they can be caught by hand. Once snipe are driven south by hard weather, which usually does not occur till January, they do not return; and although a few may have weathered wintry conditions, the great majority will have gone south, not to return until the urge of Spring calls them once more to northern lands to breed.

CHAPTER XVI

HAND-REARED WILD-DUCK (1)

Early Days

GENERALLY SPEAKING WILDFOWL are the property of the rough shoot, and give occasional shots when one is after snipe. At other times they are to be got when flighting at dawn and dusk, or by the wildfowler on the coast with punt or shoulder gun. The sport calls for much patience and endurance, and is very precarious, sometimes good, often indifferent or worse, and generally disappointing. Such at least is the writer's experience of wildfowl shooting in the British Isles. But I have done very little of it, and so am not qualified to dogmatise. I am well aware, however, that the votaries of wild-fowling assign it a high place in the category of sport, preferring it to any other kind of shooting, particularly when geese are the quarry, and welcoming hardship and discomfort from gales and wintry weather, such conditions being the most favourable for their favourite sport. But one should serve one's apprenticeship to wild-fowling when young, and I admit that years ago I was spoiled for this sport by getting the cream of duck-shooting in India.

Imagine yourself in a flat-bottomed punt which has been shoved well into the rushes; or better still, clad in khaki shirt and shorts, standing knee-deep in water pleasantly warmed by the sun's rays, while in a blue and cloudless sky every kind of duck is driven over you at varying heights, sometimes in twos and threes, sometimes singly, and sometimes in companies of fifty or more. Picture yourself firing until your gun is too hot to hold, even with a glove, and you have recourse to dipping your smoking barrels in water to cool them, and finding at the end of a half an hour that you have expended 200 cartridges for 50 head of duck of every variety, pintail, mallard, widgeon, gadwall, several kinds of pochard and two varieties of teal, to say nothing of the occasional, and sometimes more than occasional, goose. That this is no fancy picture will be readily attested by anyone who has participated in duck drives in Sind, the Punjab, or the United Provinces, and in other parts of India. For the glorious and all-too-fleeting ten days of your cold-weather leave you will have enjoyed this sort of shooting, sometimes better, sometimes worse, interspersed with trudges after snipe and black partridge, that prince of Eastern game-birds. And always under a blue sky, with a nip in the air in the early morning that went to your head like wine. Alas! we have deliberately surrendered our heritage, and for our race at least the old Pagoda-tree will blossom never again.

But I would not be thought to infer that because a man has had good shooting abroad he is apt to despise small bags else-where. Far from it. A good sportsman is thankful for what the gods are pleased to provide, and he is just as happy in shooting a couple of widgeon or teal under difficult weather conditions of flighting at home as when assisting to fill the bag in a big duck-shoot in India. It is not the spirit that is unwilling, but the flesh that is weak. After years spent in the tropics, the retired Anglo-Indian—to use a maladroit term sanctioned by long usage—is no longer young. His blood has become thin, and bouts of fever have left their mark. He cannot now brave with impunity the "winter and rough weather" which are the inevitable concomitants of wild-fowling in the British Isles.

I can, however, strongly recommend the rearing of wild-duck as a less strenuous form of duck-shooting to those who have not tried it, and who own or are able to rent the necessary water. By wild-duck is meant the mallard, and only the mallard. None of the others will breed in captivity, and have moreover to be pinioned to prevent their migrating in due season. If only the teal would adapt itself to hand-rearing what splendid sport it would afford! Far better than the mallard, for the teal, while flying very swiftly, sticks close to favoured localities, circling its haunts when shot at, and flying to and fro until finally driven off. Even then it is quite likely to return when peace once more succeeds disturbance. However, as the teal declines to lend itself to domestication in any form, we have to put up with the wild-duck or mallard as a substitute, and a very efficient one it makes. There are, however, two drawbacks to the wild-duck as a provider of sport. One is that your hand-reared bird may refuse to fly after the first attempt, flopping down into the pond or lake as soon as possible, and defeating all efforts to induce it to rise again; the other is exactly the opposite. Having risen, and having learnt what it means to be shot at, the duck proceed to mount into the heavens forthwith, and after the first few minutes every bird may be hundreds of feet high and finally depart to more peaceful waters until nightfall. These difficulties can be overcome, the first almost entirely, as explained later on; while the second depends to some extent on the accessibility of more ponds or lakes, but chiefly on the patience and good sense of the shooters. If they shoot at duck too high to kill, they are only ruining their own sport, and that of others by keeping the birds up. Whereas, if left alone for a few minutes, the duck will gradually return and give sporting shots as they wheel round preparatory to alighting in their sanctuary.

But I am rather putting the cart before the horse, and counting my ducklings before they are hatched, or rather before the eggs are procured. For this is the first step, and a most important one it is. The eggs *must* be from pure wild stock. If there is the slightest mixture of tame blood the duck will never fly well. Having procured the eggs, which are best picked up from the fens if this can be arranged with other owners, the rest is simple if the necessary water is available, as to which more anon. Wild-duck are much easier to rear than pheasants if a few necessary precautions are taken, and much cheaper, or they were before the war, and presumably will be again. The chief enemies of ducklings are, first and foremost rats, sun, and, strangely enough, water, which gives them cramp until they are from six to eight weeks old. Water they must have to drink, and plenty of it, but the receptacles should be too narrow for them to get into. When introduced to the pond or lake which is to be their future home, pike if of any size will prove most destructive; and by night lines and every other means these pests should be exterminated as far as possible before the ducklings are introduced. Once they can fly, this, and practically all other dangers, disappear.

The eggs having been procured are placed under fowls.

138

Sometimes a hen disliking the appearance of ducklings instead of chickens will kill all her brood as soon as hatched. This is unusual, but when eggs are chipping it is advisable when possible to watch the behaviour of the hen as the ducklings make their appearance, and if she shows any signs of animosity the brood should be distributed among other hens of kinder nature. The ducklings' staple food consists of special duck-meal manufactured in three grades according to their age. It is not proposed to go into details as to the feeding and general management of wild-duck, since specific instructions will be found in a booklet on the subject issued by the manufacturers, but mention must be made of certain matters which are necessary to success. Before dealing with these, however, it may be said that since the meal has only to be mixed with cold water and stirred into a thick paste, the rearing of wild-duck up to the age of 5 or 6 weeks is a far simpler matter than rearing pheasants; and that once the necessary pens are in place, to rear four or five hundred is very little more trouble than to rear fifty.

It seems absurd not to give ducklings water to splash about in, when in the wild state the mother duck takes her brood with impunity on to the river or lake within a few hours of their being hatched. Keepers will tell you that the wild-duck never keeps her ducklings on the water for any length of time. This may be so, but they must at any rate be perpetually dabbling for food in wet places. I believe that immunity from cramp in the wild state is simply due to the duck constantly brooding her young, and as they nestle under her warm feathers they dry very quickly, and so come to no harm. Then in a very short time the ducklings get so used to the cold water that it has no effect on them. That this is so, is shown by the fact that when hand-reared wild-ducklings are introduced to a pond at six weeks, several will be seized with cramp after a few hours and shortly die. But after twenty-four hours there will be few if any more seizures, and at the end of forty-eight hours none.

If the introduction to their permanent home is postponed until the ducklings are eight weeks old there will probably be no losses from cramp, but to deprive them for another two weeks of their natural element, and the insect food which is so necessary to their well-being, is to court other dangers which may be worse than a few deaths from cramp. Disease may break out, and unless the ducklings are shifted from time to time on to fresh ground, and are given a substitute for the insect food their systems crave, a bad outbreak of feather-plucking may ensue. This is to be dreaded for it is difficult to stop, and is most infectious; that is to say the bad example spreads like wild-fire, and unless checked immediately there will hardly be a duckling which has not lost some of its wing quills. This will throw the shooting season back six weeks or two months according to the extent of the outbreak, thus adding greatly to the rearing expenses, besides providing unlimited opportunities for poaching, and upsetting all one's plans.

The way feather-plucking starts is as follows: the ducklings are all in need of insect food or its equivalent as soon as their feathers begin to grow, say from a month to five weeks. Whether by instinct or by mere chance, two or three of the most forward ones will have discovered that the soft quills of the wings contain blood at the root. They are too sensible to pull their own feathers out—a painful operation judging from the squeaks of the victims—when they can operate with impunity on the quills of their fellows. Accordingly they attack any youngster within reach. There is a dash at a passing duckling, a grab at the wing, a squeak of dismay and pain from the victim which scuttles to temporary safety, while the male-factor gobbles up the tasty morsel in a trice, and at once looks out for more. The bad example is immediately followed, and there is constant commotion in the pens as pursued and pursuers rush about, the former in a vain attempt to escape, and the latter intent on a juicy meal.

The remedy is (1) to avoid overcrowding. (2) To provide in addition to the duck-meal, the insides of rabbits chopped up, or earthworms, or finely-chopped raw meat. Some substitute for insect food they must have daily, or the trouble will continue. (3) The malefactors must be immediately segregated, and should have a liberal allowance of some kind of raw meat. (4) At the earliest opportunity the ducklings should be taken to their permanent home. At the risk of a few deaths from cramp, I am personally in favour of placing the ducklings on the water at six weeks. It is most noticeable how from this moment all feather-plucking ceases. The ducklings are fully-occupied in snapping at the duns and spinners which congregate on fresh water, and in diving for nymphs and worms. They get unlimited insect food, and in consequence thrive amazingly, and forget their bad habits.

A large sheet of water is unnecessary. Two hundred duck can be kept in perfect health on a pond not greatly exceeding a quarter of an acre in extent. But it must be fed from a stream or spring, and preferably the first as producing a far greater supply of insect food. The word pond rather denotes a village pond—a bare circular bit of water, stagnant and uninteresting. The pond for wild-duck should be entirely different. It should have overhanging trees to give shade and privacy, and if it is irregular in shape with miniature islands or clumps of rushes so much the better. If a stream runs through the property it is a simple matter to fence it off with wire-netting and stakes, and lead the water off to form a pond so that the ducklings will have access to the pond, and to that portion of the stream that lies between the wire-netting fences. If a pond is dug, the sides must be revetted with planks or they will gradually fall in, as the ducks nibble away the earth for worms and frogs, and for the sheer pleasure of doing so. Gorse and willow should be planted here and there round the pond, but it should not be entirely surrounded, as duck hate to feel shut in and unable to see what is happening about them. I do not recommend either rhododendrons or brambles. Both grow apace and soon become impenetrable. The water should be quite shallow; a foot to fifteen inches is ample, and slatted planks should be placed at intervals round the sides, to enable the ducklings to clamber out on to the banks.

A rat- and fox-proof pen should be erected at the waterside for night use until the ducklings are able to fly. Some coops should be placed inside, and the ducklings herded into the pen at dusk. They soon learn to use the coops if it comes on to rain. At first they should be kept in the pen until the rays of the morning sun strike the water, but as they grow older and become inured to the chill of running water they can be released earlier.

If there is another pond or small sheet of water on the property it is a great asset, for the duck will keep in the vicinity in the endeavour to alight on one or the other, thus affording better sport.

Before discussing how to make the duck fly, a word must be said about poaching. Of all the dangers to which wild ducklings are liable, the human poacher is by far the worst. He bides his time until the ducklings are almost fully grown, but are still in the flapper stage, and while they are still unsophisticated and unsuspecting. Then he comes down some dark night perhaps with a pal, and a well-trained lurcher, and sends the dog round to drive the duck towards him. Meanwhile he and his friend have their weighted net ready, and as the duck swim towards them the net is cast by the light of a torch, and twenty or thirty duck are struggling in its folds. Their necks are speedily wrung, and the two beauties quickly depart to await their next opportunity some ten days later, after the hue and cry has died down, and the duck have partially recovered from their fright. Unless the keeper's cottage is close by, the only preventive that is likely to be at all effective is to install a trustworthy man as night watcher, who may or may not be a keeper, to sleep or rather to rest in a small tent or hut close to the pond from the time the duck are table size until they have learned to fly really well, and to spring up at the slightest alarm. (Another reason for having nothing but pure wild blood.) The watcher should have an alert dog with him, and be provided with a loud whistle and a powerful torch. Whether he should be armed would depend on circumstances, but if not, he should certainly carry a stout cudgel. But it will probably be found that his torch and whistle will prove adequate to all occasions, since his object is to identify rather than to effect a capture, which, if he is alone, might prove a difficult matter. He should wait until the poacher or poachers are fairly committed, and if he then flashes his torch and blows his whistle loudly, he will have the satisfaction of seeing them run like hares, but not, it is to be hoped, before he has identified them.

The night watcher would probably be required for two months from about mid-June to the middle of August, although vigilance cannot be altogether relaxed even then. The man should have opportunity for sleeping in the daytime in order to keep awake at night.

143

The help of the police will be invaluable in ascertaining the bad characters of the neighbourhood if not already known. Their appearance should be well known to the watcher, with a view to making identification easy if one or more of them should be tempted to raid the pond.

It may be asked, why go to the expense of installing a night watcher when one is not found necessary, or at any rate feasible, for hand-reared pheasants? But the two cases are not analogous. Pheasants stray; hand-reared wild-duck do not, if they are regularly fed. There is no certainty where pheasants will be roosting—they may be in half a dozen places in the same wood, or in adjacent woods. To guard them adequately half a dozen watchers would be needed. But duck stick to the same piece of water, unless, of course, they have a whole length of stream to wander in. And they sleep fifty and more huddled up in a bunch. It is the easiest thing in the world to net them wholesale while they are in the flapper stage. I know, for I have suffered from poachers' depredations. And one man can adequately guard the lot. It seems a penny-wise and pound-foolish policy to risk the loss of months of work and splendid sport for the sake of fifteen to twenty pounds which is about what the extra pay of a night watcher for two months would amount to. .

CHAPTER XVII

HAND-REARED WILD-DUCK (2)

The Final Stage

ONCE THE DUCKLINGS can fly a little they should be fed farther and farther away from the pond and if possible up-hill. (Their food for some time back now will have been entirely of grain.) A horn should be used for calling them, and they will soon learn to waddle up-hill for a quarter of a mile or even more until right away from the pond. After they have been fed they should be flushed by the keeper and his assistant who have remained hidden, rushing at them with flapping cloths in their hands, or by a dog turned loose upon them. By hook or by crook they must be made to fly. The hill will help them in their downward flight, for they will make straight for the pond. Duck soon get too tame, and they *must* be kept wild. For this reason the dog, a trained retriever, should not be *en évidence* while the duck are being fed or they will get used to it. If the men unaided can flush the duck, which will nearly always be the case, the dog is best left out of the proceedings,

10

for it will be needed at a later stage, and the duck must regard it as an enemy. In due course the birds on hearing the horn will fly to the sound, and a pretty sight it is. They should not always be fed in the same place, but invariably at a distance from the pond, which they should be taught to regard as a sanctuary. There should be no whistling to them or anything of that sort while they are feeding, and the subsequent flushing must never be omitted. Once they get their flight feathers they soon become strong on the wing, and after a time will fly to the pond of their own accord after feeding, but it is better to flush them, as it helps to defeat the poachers' machinations, as well as keeping them wild.

After the duck have learned to fly readily and are fairly strong on the wing, it is a very good plan to flash a torch on them on a dark night, and to set the dog on them as they are resting on the water and on the edge of the pond. They will hate flying at night at first, but after they have had two or three frights of the kind, they will readily take to wing on finding that the dog chases them in their own element. The object of this is twofold. To get them to rise from the water, and to safeguard them against poachers. It is possible that in these experiments a few duck may be lost, but it is better to lose three or four now than ten times that number, or even more, by the poacher's net.

However many ponds or lakes there may be, one should always be kept as a sanctuary. On shooting days the guns should never be placed round this water, but well away. The duck fly round in a wide sweep, and give grand shots as they come over the trees. If the guns are placed within sight of the water the duck are much more likely to desert the locality for other water perhaps a mile or more distant, not belonging to the shoot. Moreover, placing guns round the principal water defeats its own object. The duck either mount into the sky and keep there, eventually seeking sanctuary elsewhere, or refuse to leave the water at all, quickly realising that so long as they stick to the water they are safe. It is, indeed, very difficult to flush duck from water in the day-time—that is hand-reared duck—and once they are allowed to settle on it, almost impossible to flush them again without the use of boats, or a strong-swimming and persistent dog. Hence the necessity of accustoming them to be flushed from land, and as far from the sanctuary as possible, and of keeping the dog as much a stranger to them as a fox would be. It is perhaps unnecessary to say that only pure wild stock are capable of continuously circling round and flying to and fro for half an hour at a time without alighting, and at a pace in no degree slower than that of their parents of the marshes. The difficulty indeed is to get them to fly low enough to shoot. As previously said, it will help to this end if there are one or more small lakes or ponds within half a mile of the sanctuary. Two or three guns should be hidden round these, so as to keep the duck constantly on the move. But the main thing is to be patient, and to avoid firing at duck practically out of range, a practice which is the ruin of any duck-shooting whether at home or abroad.

The shooting should take place in the evening at the usual feeding hour or a little earlier. The duck should be called by horn to a distance and there flushed, and this procedure should be carried out also at the same time at the other pieces of water should any duck be on them. The guns must be hidden wherever they are placed, or the duck will soon learn to avoid them. A few men with large white flags on high poles, eight or nine feet high—the higher the better so long as they are not too heavy to be waved—should be posted round the pond or

147

ponds. The flags should be used with discrimination. While the duck are flying high the flags should be furled and the operators should take cover under trees or in bracken and keep perfectly still. But they must also keep a sharp look-out so as not to be taken unawares. As soon as a duck is seen heading for the sanctuary with the obvious intention of settling, the nearest flagman must jump up and vigorously wave his flag. The result will be that the duck or ducks will swerve upwards and away, and probably make for the farther water where they will receive similar treatment. Once they are allowed to settle they will be most difficult to flush again. The ordinary flankers' flags as used in grouse shooting are practically useless. The material should be coarse calico 3 feet square, and must be on long light poles of hazel or similar wood, the thinner, within reason, the better, as the flags must be waved vigorously. Experiments should be made on these lines twice before the actual shoot; at intervals of at least ten days, since the duck must not get accustomed to the use of the flags, or they will learn to disregard them.

It is perhaps unnecessary to say that experiments should not be attempted until the duck are really strong on the wing. Without practice in flying they will easily tire, and then nothing will keep them from settling. Indeed they will be too exhausted to continue to fly. The first shoot if possible should not take place until after the duck are observed to flight in the evening, and sometimes in the day-time, of their own accord, flying backwards and forwards over the trees at a good height often for twenty minutes at a time obviously from sheer joy of being on the wing. No half- or quarter-bred stock will be found to behave like this.

Curiously enough, while shots fired at them while in the air tend to keep them high, hand-reared duck seem to pay no attention to shots fired in order to flush them, or to prevent their settling. It is always unsafe to dogmatise from one's own experience, but I have found shots fired with the object mentioned perfectly useless. Probably duck are used to hearing shots at rabbits, pigeons, and later at partridges, and pay no attention to them, though they soon discover when they themselves are being shot at. In the first experiments, firing in the air was tried to keep them from settling but without the slightest effect. So flags were substituted and proved entirely successful. Elsewhere I have seen shots fired at low-flying hand-reared wild-duck in the endeavour to prevent them from settling, and though the duck fired at were killed it had no effect on the others, which promptly made a rush for the water and there remained.

On the face of it, it does seem cruel to rear duck and thereafter betray their confidence by shooting them, but if they are kept wild—and they can be by the exercise of a little care—it is no more cruel than to rear and shoot pheasants. Indeed, kinder very often, for pure-bred wild-duck will at any rate fly high, and so present difficult shots, whereas, unless forced to, the pheasant prefers to use its legs rather than its wings, and in consequence, in the absence of special measures, often gives as sorry an exhibition of the power of flight as it is possible to imagine. But after all is said, is not the confidence of the farmyard fowl abused? These poor things get very little fun out of their short lives, and even their eggs are rifled for the benefit of man, while the manner of their death is pitiful in the extreme. So I think we shooters can look those moralists fairly in the face, who, in spite of their outcry against blood sports, eat fowls and ducks and their eggs with avidity, and concern themselves not at all with the manner of the victims' death, and still less of their lives.

149

All the same I must admit that I hated shooting my hand-reared duck, although I had no compunction in shooting duck reared elsewhere. Wild-ducklings are extraordinarily attractive little creatures, full of brains and character. After one has fed and tended them and watched them disporting themselves in the water to which they have been introduced, to shoot them seems almost a crime, however wild one may have succeeded in making them eventually. So on shooting days I usually contented myself in superintending proceedings, and with the help of my Labrador, retrieving duck that had fallen in thickets and places in which, but for canine assistance, they would never have been found. I should feel the same compunction in shooting partridges that I had personally reared, but pheasants would not appeal to me in the same way. I should have no qualms about shooting them whether I had nursed them from the egg stage or not, especially if they were good high birds. Have gamekeepers any qualms on the subject I wonder? I imagine not. What they hate is to see their birds missed, especially when they have been at pains to show good ones, and in this they have all my sympathy. One sometimes hears of unscrupulous keepers flushing pheasants in large numbers, not from any sympathy with the pheasants, but merely in order to have more to show another time. But this is hardly likely to occur without the connivance of the owner, whether of a private shoot or of a syndicate. In any case the responsibility is his.

But to return to our hand-reared wild-duck. A word of caution regarding the actual shooting may be necessary. The sport should not be unduly prolonged. If the duck are affording good shots, flying at a good sporting height and coming down from the high heavens at frequent intervals, the proceedings should be closed after half an hour at the latest, before any duck have settled in the sanctuary. If they are made to fly until exhausted they will settle—indeed they must—in spite of the waving of all the flags in Christendom, and they will refuse to fly again. Once having learnt to brave the flags they will do so readily in future shoots which will be ruined in consequence—a disaster to be carefully guarded against. After all, the poor things have only been flying for a month or so, and even the wild-duck of the marshes, except when flighting or migrating, does not fly for long spells without a rest.

The gun I would personally prefer to use on strong-flying duck, and on high pheasants would be the ordinary 12-bore game gun, with either the right barrel three-quarter choke and the left full choke, or with both barrels full choke, and bored to take $1\frac{1}{16}$ oz. of No. 5 shot.

An oncoming high duck should not be fired at until the bird is over the shooter's head, thus allowing the shot to penetrate through the feathers, rather than to strike against them. Many duck are lost by being shot at too soon, when the density of the breast feathers readily resists penetration if the bird is at any height.

As previously stated three or four hundred duck can be kept in perfect health on a sheet of water less than an acre in extent, given suitable conditions such as shady trees and moving water, however slow. If fed by a stream, a simple form of weir is desirable, if not absolutely necessary, to keep the water in the pond at the proper level.

But there is one great drawback to keeping duck on a piece of water, small in proportion to their numbers, and that is the extraordinary animosity of wild-duck to ducklings other than their own. They will breed readily, and have no objection to nesting in close proximity to each other. But once the ducklings are hatched it is quite another story. To us, all wild ducklings of the same age look alike, but each duck knows her own brood, and if an unfortunate duckling from another brood happens to pass within a few yards, it is instantly attacked and killed in a matter of seconds. One would suppose that the mother of the duckling attacked would come to the rescue, but in my experience she never does. On the contrary if she herself unwittingly brings her brood within range, so to speak, of another duck which also has a family, this duck as likely as not, will sail out and attack, not the trespasser, but her inoffensive offspring, one after the other, killing each in turn, while the brood of the murderess paddles unconcernedly in her wake. Meanwhile, the bereft mother takes herself off, followed by the one or two remaining ducklings who have saved themselves by scuttling to a safe distance, while their brothers and sisters were being done to death. In the same way she will herself attack other broods that invade her territory. And so internecine warfare is being constantly waged with disastrous results. The only remedy—frequently an impossible one—is more space. On a large expanse of water ducks with families can avoid the proximity of others similarly situated, while the ducklings are small. After three or four weeks they appear to be immune, or possibly are better able to make their escape when attacked. Full-grown ducks, too, will fight among themselves, but I do not remember ever to have seen matrons so engage. These battles generally take place in the breeding season, and are doubtless the result of jealousy, when two young ducks are making up to the same drake. They hang on to a wing like bulldogs, and do their best to drown each other, fortunately without success.

This slaughter of the innocents is really serious, and is all the more annoying in that it comes after the shooting season is over, when there is plenty of room for the now depleted stock if only the mothers of families were more tolerant of others in like case. Two or three small ponds do not help matters here, as duck generally favour one to the exclusion more or less of the others; and in any case the same thing will take place on any of them. If a considerable length of stream, or a lake with islets and inlets is not available, a fresh supply of eggs must be purchased each year, placed under fowls, and the ducklings hand-reared as before. In fact, all the trouble is to do again—a great pity, as except for her intolerance of the young of others, and her passive acquiescence in the massacre of her own, the wild-duck is an excellent mother. Proof of this is afforded by the persistent way in which she will feign disablement in order to lure a human being from the vicinity of her brood hiding in the rushes.

It would be reasonable to suppose that this aversion to the young of other ducks of the same species, and the apparent unconcern of the duck whose brood is attacked, is a provision of nature to prevent overcrowding. The inherited instinct of the hand-reared wild-duck would function, irrespective of whether there was need for it or not. But there are two factors militating against this theory. The first is that the wild-duck of rivers, fens and marshes, has ample room in which to breed in absolute seclusion and, as far as I know, always does so. There is, therefore, no reason for an aggressive instinct to survive, whether such an instinct may or may not have been acquired originally in course of evolution. And the second factor is the absolute overcrowding that occurs among certain sea-birds such as gulls, gannets, guillemots, and others, during the nesting season. And we have rookeries and heronries, both greatly overcrowded to all appearance. Nature apparently approves; at any rate she has implanted no instinct against it. Much as I like the mallard, I am afraid we must put these aggressive onslaughts down to sheer jealousy. The more unnatural, one would suppose, in that the wild-duck is naturally gregarious, and, except in the breeding season, swims and sleeps in company often in large numbers. But however we may account for it, the fact remains that hand-reared wild-duck will kill each other's young on slight provocation. In the absence of rats and pike a few families may survive on small areas; but without access to a length of stream, or a large extent of water, numerous nurseries are out of the question.

If, by the way, it is hoped to breed from hand-reared mallard, moorhens—or waterhens as they are sometimes called —should be kept down, for they are inveterate egg-suckers. Finding broken eggs in two or three nests with the yolk gone except for yellow smears over the unbroken eggs, I suspected rats, although we had done our best to exterminate these pests. Next morning before dawn I was down at the pond, where several duck were nesting in high clumps of rushes, and took up a hidden position within easy shot. As it grew light a moorhen flew on to a duck's nest much to my surprise, and I watched it give two or three stabs, and then hold its head up, rather in the manner of a connoisseur sampling a good glass of wine. Here I thought it time to interfere, and as I showed myself it flew off; I shot it just as it reached the bank of the stream. Its beak when I picked it up was covered with yolk. This was not an isolated case, as I subsequently discovered. Thereafter war was declared on all moorhens in the vicinity, and thenceforward there were no more broken eggs. One of the marauders had built a nest under a clump of rushes on the top of which a duck was sitting. So cleverly was the nest hidden that I only discovered it by chance. I had waded into the pond to examine some nests, when a moorhen flew out from a clump of rushes I was just approaching. The duck's nest was the usual depression in the clump and was deserted, two eggs having been broken and the contents sucked. But there was no sign of the moorhen's nest, and I knew that it had not flown from the top of the clump. Hardly expecting to find anything, I bent down and lifted a mass of rushes which were overhanging with their tips in the water. Right underneath the rushes was a moorhen's nest with eight eggs in it, almost touching the water, a cunningly chosen spot because so absolutely concealed. In the light of my experience of a day or two earlier, and with the evidence of the broken eggs to confirm it, I had no hesitation in removing the nest of the despoiler, eggs and all. I shot another moorhen a day or two later which may have been this bird. At any rate there was no recurrence of the trouble.

I used to regard the moorhen as a pleasing feature of the countryside, a picturesque accessory to our streams and meres, though I cannot say that I ever admired its skulking habits. But it looks so innocent as it jerks its way to the harbourage of the waterside, flirting its white tail as it bobs in and out of the rushes, that from its appearance no one would believe it to be the malefactor it undoubtedly is. I know it now for a pestilent egg-sucker, a despoiler of other birds' homes without a shadow of excuse. It is, moreover, an avid devourer of trout spawn. It has not even the redeeming merit of affording sport, and so finds a prominent place on my black-list in company with the hooded crow and the magpie, the latter a handsome villain of the deepest dye. The waterhen may flirt its tail to its heart's content: it will never make me believe in its innocence again.

FIRST FLIGHT

When Autumn brings a warning chill,
   And fleeing Summer's still in sight,
It may be yours to sense a thrill
   On seeing duck in evening flight,
And finding, as in wid'ning rings
   They mount, that these are yours, once tame,
But now with wild blood in their wings
   Domesticated but in name.
Now clearly seen against the sky,
   Now swallowed up in murk of night,
In silent ecstasy they fly,
   Rejoicing in their new-found might.

Contentment may be yours—and yet
Hard on its heels will come regret.

CHAPTER XVIII

MISCELLANEOUS. SMALL FRY: VERMIN: POACHERS: KEEPERS

Wood Pigeon

TAKE IT BY AND LARGE, the wood pigeon is, except on occasion, an unsatisfactory bird from a sporting point of view, and the farmer would give it a stronger label on account of the damage it does to his turnips and kale. From its numbers the wood pigeon would provide excellent sport if only it would fly within range of the ordinary game-gun, and if it were not so extraordinarily wary. Good sport can be had when pigeons frequent a wood to feed on acorns and beechmast, if the shooter is well concealed; but the wood must be kept quiet for ten days or a fortnight before shooting takes place, otherwise the pigeons will keep so high that comparatively few will be brought to bag. A high wind, foggy weather, or a hard frost are all favourable for this sport. Decoys placed head to wind help the bag. Where pigeon are in the habit of raiding root crops in numbers, sport, varying from fair to very good, is obtainable if well camouflaged pits are dug and left unoccupied for two or three days to allow the birds to get used to them. Sometimes very excellent sport is to be had when pigeon come in to roost, but here again the wood must have been undisturbed for several days or sport will be poor.

Outside these special opportunities the wood pigeon is a disappointing bird, and a great waster of time and cartridges. Where occasional shots are fairly frequent the gun to use is a full-choke pigeon gun taking the $2\frac{3}{4}$-in. cartridge with $1\frac{1}{2}$ oz. No. 5 shot. But this would not be a suitable weapon if a number of shots were expected to be fired within a short space of time. A heavily-choked game-gun taking the ordinary $2\frac{1}{2}$-in. case loaded with $1\frac{1}{16}$ oz. of No. 5 or 6 shot would, if available, be my selection for any occasion when fifty to a hundred or more shots were expected to be fired within an hour or two. Unfortunately, most men have on these occasions to use the ordinary game-gun, giving as a rule a much more open pattern, at any rate from the right barrel, than one would prefer to use on high pigeon.

Not only does the wood pigeon habitually fly high but it is for its size extraordinarily tough. Opinions differ as to whether this is due to excessive vitality or to density of plumage; but the fact remains that a wood pigeon will carry on after receiving shot that would crumple up a grouse. Especially is this the case if it is hit in the breast.

I am sure that it is a mistake to fire at pigeon while waiting for pheasants at a covert-shoot. Those random shots, so seldom productive of result, must induce many a wily old cock pheasant to turn back over the beaters' heads when flushed later on. Why advertise your presence, and more important, the presence of your fellow-guns, before you need? And to fire at a pigeon, or for the matter of that at a hare, before a partridge drive is little short of a crime. An obvious truism, one might suppose, yet one sees it done frequently, and not always by novices either.

THE RAIDERS

'Tis pleasant in full-blossomed Spring
To hear the cushat's murmuring
   Borne softly on the breeze,
Blending in perfect unison
With bird-song welcoming the dawn,
   And sights as fair as these.

The dew on grass like beads of pearls,
The cloudless sky the mist unfurls
   Proclaim a perfect day;
While gossamer spun overnight
By fairies in the bright starlight
   Floats tardily away.

Alas! that I should have to harm
This picture of fair Nature's charm
   (Dame Nature at her best);
But truth compels me here to state
The cushat with her cooing mate
   Is a most dreadful pest.

I love to hear them in the Spring
Cooing away like anything,
   Well-hidden in the trees;
But oh! I hate the ravages
They make upon my cabbages,
   My turnip tops and peas.

I own I'm weak, but cannot bring
Myself to shoot them in the Spring
   (And don't they know it too!)
But when the Autumn brings by scores
Vile foreigners upon these shores
   I make no more ado.

Not that I with well-loaded gun
Achieve a vast amount of fun,
    Or wipe out past insults;
So high they fly, so swift they turn,
That I a deal of powder burn
    For very small results.

In short to end this halting rhyme
The pigeons beat me every time.

Hares

As I do not shoot hares I am afraid I can say little about them, except to beg my readers, if they must shoot them, to aim well ahead, and to refrain from taking long shots. Thirty yards should be regarded as the extreme range for a straight going-away hare, and five yards farther if crossing. While it is difficult to miss a hare altogether, owing to its size, it is extremely easy to wound it instead of making a clean kill, and it is horrible to think of the poor thing getting away wounded. Yet it is no uncommon thing to see men in a partridge drive when loaded with No. 6 or No. 7 shot firing up to fifty yards at a going-away hare.

Good shots in particular ought to abstain from so cruel a proceeding, since a hare at this distance can only be bagged by the merest fluke, but must inevitably receive a number of pellets, and probably escapes to die a lingering death, or most likely to fall a prey to prowling vermin. Where hares are numerous, and are doing damage they have to be thinned out, but it is execution rather than sport. Poor puss has a free pass where I am concerned. She is so confiding, and presents such an easy mark, that it affords me more satisfaction to watch her go off unharmed than to shoot at her. I take no credit for this abstention. It gives me no pleasure to shoot a hare, and I refrain, therefore, from doing so.

TO A HARE

Oh fur-clad shape of russet hue
   In furrow shrinking,
This verse I dedicate to you,
   To you I'm drinking. . . .
Long may you live to sip the dew
   When sun is sinking.

How sad your plight that foes abound
   For your undoing;
Above, and on, and under ground
   There's mischief brewing:
And man equipped with gun and hound
   There's no eschewing.

Why should he try to bring about
   Your dissolution?
The answer is comprised, no doubt,
   In evolution;
Some atavistic urge cries out
   For red solution.

Primeval impulse in the blood
  Prompts man to kill;
Of old he hunted you for food
  And does so still;
And tho' the need has gone for good,
  Remains the thrill.

Most other game on shooter's skill
  Makes high demand;
Snipe, grouse, or partridges at will
  Are all to hand:
Then leave poor Jack, and better, Jill,
  Upon the land.

Few sportsmen find it pleasant now
  To shoot a hare;
One might as well shoot grazing cow
  For skill that's there;
Poor Puss fares badly, anyhow,
  From poacher's snare.

Here's one last health to all your race,
  Whate'er betide!
May nothing check your speedy pace,
  Your gallant stride. . . .
Long may you live to breed, and grace
  Our countryside.

Rabbits

Rabbits are another matter. I shoot a rabbit at every opportunity: they are not far removed from vermin, and frequently give most sporting shots. A rabbit put up on the hillside or in an open field, should be a gift for the gun, but when scuttling from burrow to burrow, dodging about in bracken, or darting across a ride it can tax the skill of the very best performer with the shot-gun. On these occasions I always try to bear in mind Charles Lancaster's advice: "Shoot not where he is, but where he is bolting to."

Ferreting can be very good fun, or the dullest and coldest form of sport imaginable. On good ground where rabbits are plentiful and burrows not too close together, and when several ferrets are used, excellent sport is afforded if the rabbits are bolting well. This they generally do in dry and windy weather, if they have not previously been unduly harried. Proceedings should be carried out as quietly as possible, and the guns should stand well away from the bolt-holes, and down-wind of the burrow. If a rabbit hears or scents human beings it will often

165

refuse to bolt, preferring to be scratched or bitten to death, rather than run the gauntlet outside.

I cannot say that I enjoy stalking rabbits with a rook rifle in summer. The actual stalking is quite good fun, but the shooting, at least to my mind, is not. If one uses a solid bullet many rabbits dive into their holes wounded, as the bullet simply passes through without breaking up. The rabbit may be hit well forward in a vital spot, but unless both forelegs are broken or it is hit in the head or neck, the chances are all in favour of its getting to ground, when it has to be dug out, should this be possible, to the detriment of the burrow, and the disturbance of its occupants.

The use of a hollow or soft-nosed bullet obviates this contingency, but makes a horrid mess of the rabbit even when hit well forward. A gory rabbit is a horrible thing to carry even for a short distance, and I have, therefore, discarded the rifle for the shot-gun. This necessitates getting to closer quarters, and often the quarry is alarmed and decamps before one can get within shot. On the other hand when bunny is surprised at some distance from hedge or burrow, he often gives a sporting shot as he makes a dash for safety. The only object of these forays is to provide meat for the dogs, and although there is no fun to be got out of a pot-shot at a rabbit with a shot-gun, still it is better to pick up a clean rabbit than one with a hole in it the size of a crown piece, and bleeding like a pig from the destructive effect of an express or soft-nose bullet. One certainly gets a mild thrill from seeing a rabbit crumple up from a well-placed bullet at sixty or seventy yards fired from a miniature rifle, but nothing like the satisfaction experienced when bunny, going all out for the safety of the hedge, turns a complete somersault as the result of a charge of No. 5 shot in the head at 35 yards distance.

166

For accurate shooting with a rook rifle at rabbits a telescopic sight is very desirable if not actually necessary. A rabbit at sixty yards seems little bigger than a fly when seen through open sights or a peepsight, and it becomes a matter of luck if the bullet strikes a vital spot; whereas with the telescopic sight the bullet can be placed through or behind the shoulder time after time.

Vermin

HERE IS MY LIST OF VERMIN. *Four-footed*: Rats, stoats, weasels, foxes, hedgehogs, poaching cats and stray dogs. *Feathered*: All the crow tribe, the little owl (occasionally), the sparrow-hawk, and the moorhen, or waterhen to give it its more appropriate name. The list requires some explanation. The first four take eggs as well as young of game. Rats are horrible brutes and should be exterminated by every possible means. The harm they do among game is great. The weasel in spite of its small size is just as bloodthirsty as the stoat, and kills for the sheer lust of killing. Both are easily trapped, and the best bait is one of their own kind, for both have cannibalistic tendencies. The game-preserver who has a good head of rabbits is fortunate, for if foxes and stoats can get an unfailing supply of rabbits, far fewer pheasants and partridges will be killed than would other-wise be the case. Stoats, indeed, prefer rabbits to any other food, and although nothing in the way of game comes amiss either to foxes or the weasel tribe, especially when they have young of their own to cater for, both will take the prey that is most easily procurable. Keepers sometimes kill rabbits and leave them outside a fox's earth, in order to save their pheasants and partridges from an untimely visit.

It may not be generally known that all our game-birds (I do not here include the woodcock or snipe) after they have been sitting for a week, will allow a wire-netting cage to be built around them without attempting to move from the nest. I have personally built such cages round pheasants (wild and hand-reared), partridges, and wild-duck, and in every case the sitting bird has taken no notice of stakes being driven in, and the netting placed round them and joined up; and in every case, also, the eggs have been hatched, and the youngsters successfully led off by the parent bird. Foxes and rats avoid these cages, presumably because they fear a trap. But why they should also be avoided by the weasel tribe which is far less cunning and suspicious, I do not know. Perhaps they are not avoided, and I have simply been lucky. The netting should be some $2\frac{1}{2}$ feet high, and the diameter of the surround about a yard. Two holes should be cut at ground-level to allow the bird to creep out and in. The top may be left uncovered. These cages, of course, are only built when the hen bird of whatever species has made her nest in a dangerous spot. Considering the exposed situation of these nests it is little short of marvellous that they should be unmolested during the lengthy period of incubation. The netting is actually no ob-stacle to small vermin, since the sitting bird must have the means of ingress and egress. In the case of partridges I have used netting with a sufficiently big mesh for this purpose. Where a partridge can creep, the biggest stoat or rat could enter with ease, but I have never known them do so. The cage, however, is really intended as a protection against foxes, and admirably it answers the purpose.

Hedgehogs are inveterate egg-stealers, but are easily trapped. A poaching cat is a terror, and sooner or later meets its well-deserved end. The wise keeper hastily inters it and maintains a discreet silence. A stray dog is almost as bad in the breeding season. If the owner is known he should be interviewed, and if the trouble does not stop, prosecuted. If ownerless, and it can be caught, the animal should be handed over to the police, or shot. If drastic action is not taken the brute will do as much damage as a fox—more in fact, for it has no instinctive fear of man, and will hunt both by day and night.

Of feathered vermin, ravens, carrion-crows, hooded-crows and magpies can be bracketed together for the mischief they do. They take both eggs and young of game, and song-birds. Ravens are fortunately scarce, for the damage they do is in proportion to their size and strength, and one might add, appetite. They will gobble up young grouse and ptarmigan when they are half-grown. The grey-backed or hooded crow is unfortunately only too plentiful on moors and open country, and being, like the magpie, a very wary bird, is difficult to trap or to shoot. In most parts of England the magpie is, if no-where rare, not unduly obtrusive, but is an extremely common bird in Ireland, occurring all over the country from north to south. I have counted as many as seventeen magpies in a flock, or rather party, for they do not keep actually in flocks as do rooks and jackdaws. Little escapes its sharp eyes, and it levies a heavy toll on the eggs and young of game and singing birds. Rooks, jackdaws, and jays, all steal eggs, and their presence should not be encouraged on a game preserve during the breeding season. The jay is a useful sentinel in the woods, and a sprinkling of them may be permitted for this reason. The jay can look after itself extremely well, and there is, therefore, no fear of exterminating this handsome robber.

Of the hawk tribe, the peregrine is the noblest of our birds of prey, but creates havoc on a grouse moor, especially in the breeding season. A peregrine has been seen to carry five grouse to its eyrie in an hour. It is fortunate for the grouse that it is comparatively rare, and for itself that it breeds in inaccessible places on precipitous cliffs, and so escapes in a great measure the attentions of the egg-collector and game-keeper alike. It would be a thousand pities if so fine a falcon were to suffer the fate that has befallen the white-tailed eagle and the osprey, which have been exterminated as resident species within comparatively recent years. The sparrow-hawk is a pitiless slayer of small birds and the young of game-birds, and if it is fairly plentiful should be kept in check. The kestrel, on the other hand, preys chiefly on mice, small rats, and beetles, and should be protected, except when a nesting pair has actually been seen to take pheasant chicks. If the marauder is shot the trouble ceases. The same may be said of owls which, with the exception of the barn owl, have occasional lapses from the paths of rectitude. The beautiful barn owl is unfortunately becoming rarer every year. From its habit of visiting human habitations it is easily shot by the ignorant and superstitious, and is considered by the average countryman as a prize when stuffed in a glass case. The little owl for long after its intro-duction was regarded as an undesirable alien, and was shot at sight by keepers and game-preservers alike. But patient watching over many parts of England, confirmed by photo-graphs and autopsy, has proved that the staple diet of the little owl consists chiefly of cockchafers and beetles, and that the young of game-birds are only very occasionally taken. Except in the case of proved evil-doers, the little owl should be shown the wise clemency accorded to the kestrel.

Last on my list, but by no means least, comes the moorhen or waterhen. In the chapter on wild-duck I have already written of this deceiver's depredations. It should be rigorously kept down where wild-duck or trout are preserved, as it sucks the eggs of the former, and devours the spawn of the latter.

PUBLIC ENEMY NO. 1

Pernicious beasts of shadowy obscurity,
Repulsive ghouls in cavernous security,
What evil prompts your all too quick maturity
   For our unrest?

You eat our food and what you leave pollute,
You steal our corn, potatoes, and our fruit,
There's nothing you disdain to spoil or loot,
   You loathsome pest!

You harbour lice and ticks and many fleas,
Spreading all kinds of horrible disease,
And manage, spite of all, with baleful ease
   To be our guest.

Old Noah lost a splendid opportunity
To liquidate for good your continuity:
Why did he let a pair from your community
   The Ark infest?

Now a suggestion comes belatedly,
To send ten million rats in wrecks to sea,
And by atomic bombing set them free
   To do their best.

Poachers

As regards human poachers—I had almost written vermin—there is little to say. There is less partridge netting done than formerly, because it is found hardly to be worth while. Bushing or staking the fields is a well-known precaution against netting. On the other hand, the motor-car has made easier the early morning shot into a covey, and has greatly facilitated the poaching of pheasants, and the netting of hares and rabbits. The co-operation of farmers is a great help in defeating the machinations of the local poacher, and it is wise policy to obtain the assistance of the police, as they know all the bad and suspicious characters in the neighbourhood. When a poaching gang comes from a nearby industrial town, they rely almost invariably on the local knowledge of resident poachers. If these gentry—there may be only one—know that the police have their eye on them, it is a great deterrent. A good keeper should make it his business to find out the bad hats and loafers of the neighbourhood. The great thing is to let a poacher know beforehand that his character is known, and that should poaching take place he will be the first to be suspected. It is here that a quiet warning from the police will be very effective. Your pot-house frequenter is perfectly useless as a keeper. No one will have any respect for him, and a keeper must be both respected and feared if he is to protect his game.

There is little more to be said on this subject. The co-operation of owner, keeper, farmers and police is the best safeguard, together with necessary vigilance on the part of the keeper or keepers. Should a poacher be caught, the game-preserver should not hesitate to prosecute. The news will spread like wildfire, and act as a salutary warning to others of the poaching fraternity.

Keepers

Wʜᴏʟᴇ ᴄʜᴀᴘᴛᴇʀs ᴄᴏᴜʟᴅ ʙᴇ written on keepers and their various duties. But boiled down it comes to this, that a good master will not be long without a good keeper. It is, of course, desirable that the owner of a shoot should know something of game-preservation and of the habits of game, but it is not absolutely essential. He may have neither the time nor inclination for it. But he must know what results to expect, and should see that he gets them. A little knowledge indeed may prove to be but a stumbling block. It would be far wiser in such a case to interfere with the keeper as little as possible, letting the latter know what is wanted, and making it clear that he will be judged by results. Whether an owner knows much or little about game, he should at any rate be a judge of character, in which case he will very soon discover the sort of man his keeper is, and will act accordingly.

A keeper's duties are necessarily multifarious, but the different branches of keepering are even more so. A keeper

174

may be required on a rough shoot, on a grouse-moor, on a partridge shoot or beat, on a pheasant and partridge shoot with hand-reared wild-duck often included, or on a pheasant shoot alone. Pheasants and duck can often be reared by the same man with some assistance, but no keeper should be expected to rear pheasants or duck in any numbers, and to look after partridges as well. The thing is impossible, but frequently tried, invariably with disastrous results so far as the partridges are concerned. Just when they need most attention, the keeper is tied to the rearing field, and the partridges are left to chance. If driven partridges are a feature of the shoot and pheasants are reared as well, a capable man should be employed to look after the former.

This is a whole-time job, at any rate from the 1st of April to the end of July, and even after that date the birds will claim his daily attention, and particularly after the corn is cut, in order that he may have a very fair notion of the number of partridges he has on his beat. His duties will begin with the destruction of vermin, and although these will require his attention all through the breeding season and beyond, March and April are the most important months. By the end of April vermin both furred and feathered should have been largely reduced, and in May searching for partridge nests should begin in earnest.

The keeper should have a sketch-map of his beat, and mark on it with a number every nest found, the corresponding number being entered on a record giving the date when the bird began to sit, the number of eggs hatched, or the cause of the destruction of the nest, as the case may be. He should visit every nest on his beat daily, of course taking care not to alarm the laying or sitting bird. Then there will be the removal or safeguarding of nests in dangerous places, and if, as is probable, the Euston system is practised, whether wholly or in part,

175

there will be the constant substitution in nests of dummy eggs for the genuine article. These will be placed under fowls, and returned to the sitting bird when chipped and ready for hatching. Moreover, there will probably be an interchange of eggs with those from other estates. Finally, the keeper may have to do some hand-rearing of partridges, if only from those nests on which the hen partridge has been destroyed, when it has, from one cause or another, not been possible to transfer the eggs to other nests.

Enough has been said to make it clear that a partridge keeper's job is no sinecure, and just as it is possible for an inexperienced or stupid man to do an infinity of harm, so is it probable that a capable and conscientious keeper will, in a single season, double the stock of partridges on an estate, unless there should be abnormally wet and bad weather at the time of hatching. The rearing of pheasants is very largely a matter of routine, but the efficient keepering of a partridge beat demands personality, intelligence, and powers of observation, in a high degree.

Other branches of keepering are just as important, that of a grouse-moor for instance; while the efficient keeper on a rough shoot must indeed be a handyman, capable of turning his hand to anything in his own line. The only reason that attention to partridges has been stressed is because it is so frequently neglected. The head keeper and his assistants are busy with the pheasants. The partridges meanwhile are at the mercy of vermin and stray dogs, and those belonging to the shepherd and agricultural labourers on the estate. It is no one's business to provide grit, dusting places, or water in a drought, or to see that pairs of old birds do not monopolise entire hedgerows and other favourable nesting sites, to the discomfiture of numerous young nesting pairs, which have perforce to nest in

THROUGH THE REEDS

IN THE SKY

more exposed and dangerous places, and may even be driven off the shoot on to other ground. All these matters and many others are too often left to chance, and so one sees on certain shoots in excellent partridge country a dwindling, or at best a stationary stock year after year, perhaps one tenth the number of partridges that the ground could easily sustain, if adequate attention had been paid to partridge requirements.

Were I a keeper, the supervision of a partridge beat would be a work of never-failing interest, however indifferently I might perform it, particularly if I knew that I was to have the driving of it afterwards; whereas the rearing of the fatted and pampered pheasant would be but a dull task in comparison.

Still, there would always be the satisfaction of seeing the chicks grow strong and healthy in response to one's efforts, and in anticipating the pleasure of showing a goodly number of really good birds on the great day—that day which is to see for good or ill, the consummation during a few short hours of the keeper's toil and trouble, hopes and fears, of the past six months. I fear we shooters often take all this for granted, and, engrossed with our sport, have little thought to spare for the keeper's anxieties. What pleasure it must give him to see full justice done to the good birds he has been at such pains to send over; and conversely, how heartbreaking to see bird after bird escape untouched, when the guns are not up to the required standard!

Can we wonder that he prefers to ensure a good proportion of his birds being shot by flushing them close to the guns, rather than that they should escape and be lost to the shoot (as he firmly believes) for ever and a day?

Nevertheless, every good keeper is at heart a sportsman, and with the slightest encouragement from his employer will do his best to put birds over the guns as high as he can make them fly. It is for us to show that the joint endeavours of the keeper and his master are not misplaced; and if we lack the facility to deal faithfully with the average high pheasant, to betake ourselves to a shooting ground as soon as may be, and there practise at clay pigeons from the high tower until the necessary skill has been acquired, and confidence restored.

POINTS OF VIEW

First Keeper:

Oh, a keeper's life is constant strife
    With wind and weather and tide,
He has to do a hundred jobs
    And the Lord knows what beside!
He has to trap, and he has to shoot,
    And to feed his pheasants now,
And he needn't be surprised if he
    Is asked to milk the cow!

Oh, a keeper's life with toil is rife,
    Without a bit of cheer,
Except when he drops in the pub
    To get a glass of beer;
He has to rise when snug he lies,
    To face the wind instead;
No comfort's here, I'm feeling queer,
    I think I'll go to bed!

Second Keeper:

A keeper's life is a fine life, like wind and weather free,
With Nature for my guide it is the only life for me;
And I wouldn't change my free life, in spite of what they say,
For any indoor kind of life with twice a keeper's pay.

Of course it has its ups and downs when Nature shows her moods,
When heavy rain at end of June wipes out fine partridge broods;
When pheasants get the gapes, or when, too wily to be caught,
Vile poachers, worse than vermin, bring the keeper's toil to nought.

But that's a gloomy picture; you must take the other side,
When partridge drives go right, and care and skill are justified;
When pheasants sail above the trees and guns perform their part,
To watch them tumbling from the sky fair warms the keeper's heart.

Or if upon a Scottish moor when walking up he sees
Young coveys strong upon the wing with "no signs of disease",
And later sees the dogs he's trained obedient to his will,
Performing like old stagers, don't you think he gets a thrill?

His multifarious duties keep him fairly on the go,
He would very quickly chuck it if he didn't love it so;
Anxieties with vigilance are part of his estate
With great responsibilities, but his reward is great.

CHAPTER XIX

SHOOTING SYNDICATES

The subject is a thorny one, and the name is ugly. But whether we like it or not syndicate shoots have come to stay, if in fewer numbers than before the war. With increased cost of living and ever-mounting rates and taxes, only the wealthy can afford to run their own shoots and invite guests to kill their birds. As in Spring, according to the poet, "a young man's fancy lightly turns to thoughts of love", so in Spring does the impoverished landowner dally with the notion of converting his shoot into a syndicate. But the dalliance is not generally of long duration. The idea is quite attractive. The members pay the piper and the owner of the shoot calls the tune. That is to say, he runs the shoot precisely as if the members were guests, with the pleasing difference that whereas formerly his shooting cost him several hundreds of pounds per annum, he now gets it for nothing. So far it is a perfectly fair arrangement. The owner has all the trouble of running the shoot (which he enjoys), and of managing the accounts and correspondence (which usually he does not). Moreover, he provides the land, without which there would be no shooting. The members, on

181

the other hand, having paid the sum asked for are relieved of all further trouble or responsibility.

But it is certainly not fair to the other members for the owner of a shoot to regard the syndicate as a source of income. Unfortunately, the temptation to do so is great, since sportsmen generally will pay sums out of all proportion to the sport obtainable, for good, or even indifferent, shooting or fishing. Fortunately competition acts as a break on acquisitiveness, and the greater the number of shooting syndicates the better for prospective members.

But there are ways of making money out of a syndicate other than overcharging the members. Setting aside, as utterly unworthy, dishonest trickeries such as advertising a certain number of pheasants to be reared when it is only intended to put down that number of eggs or less, and trusting to wild pheasants, if any, to make up the difference, there are less reprehensible methods, the chief of which may almost be said to be hallowed by custom, such fools we mortals be! I allude to the far too general practice of showing low-flying pheasants, sometimes from sheer ignorance, but chiefly with a view to ensuring that they provide easy shooting, and so become available for the market. There is nothing inherently unfair in this practice, if the owner has allowed for the amount his dead pheasants will bring in, when charging the members a round sum on their joining the syndicate. At the best one can only say that to show "bad" birds intentionally is poor policy. But it is manifestly unfair, when calculating the amount to be charged to individual members of the syndicate, to ignore the very considerable sum to be derived from the sale of dead game. At a conservative estimate of 5s. a bird, even if only 1,000 pheasants are killed, this amounts to £250, and in favourable circumstances, as, for instance, after a war, when there is likely to be a scarcity of pheasants, the market rate may be as much as 7s. 6d. for a cock pheasant, and 6s. 6d. for a hen.

Partridges are more or less an incalculable factor, but every owner of shooting knows pretty well the number of hand-reared pheasants he has, and the approximate numbers of wild birds, and if he deducts 20 per cent for losses he should be well on the right side.

It may be urged that there is always the chance of the syndicate not filling up. I can only say that I have been a member of several shooting syndicates in my time, and I have never known a good one to be short of its full complement of members. It might possibly be so for the first year, but not after, except in case of war or other incalculable catastrophe of the kind.

In plain terms it comes to this. Is the owner of a shooting syndicate embarking on a financial speculation? Or does he propose merely to get his fair share of shooting, while running the syndicate to the best of his ability for the benefit of the other members? In the second case, his efforts are deserving of the support which they will undoubtedly receive. As to the first, such a syndicate is best avoided for obvious reasons.

But when all is said or done, we members, or prospective members of shooting syndicates, have the remedy for "bad" birds in our own hands. If one and all declined to join a syndicate in which low birds were the order of the day, matters would very soon improve. It may seem a strange thing to say at the present day when shooting at driven birds has been in vogue for nearly a century, but the maintenance of a proper standard of sportsmanship is chiefly, if not entirely, a matter of education. No big-game hunter of experience would think of

183

shooting a female or an immature male, unless absolutely necessary in order to feed his followers. What sportsman would shoot a hare in its form, or a pheasant, unless a wounded bird, on the ground? We leave such practices to other nations, whose ideals of sportsmanship are so much lower than those held by Englishmen, or so we say, with that pleasing insularity which endears us so greatly to the foreigner. What then becomes of our vaunted superiority when we deliberately shoot pheasants blundering up at our toes or not far from them, and in any case long before the unfortunate bird has a chance to get up speed, and when it is as easy to hit as any barn-door fowl? We can hardly afford to throw stones at our neighbours across the Channel or elsewhere, while our own ideals of sportsmanship are often so very brittle.

But I imagine I can hear the landowner who is running a syndicate shoot, and (or) his keeper—especially the keeper— protesting that if high birds were shown only one or two guns would be able to stop them, and that they would go on to his neighbour's ground and be wiped out, to the detriment alike of the shoot and of the owner's pocket. I believe these fears to be absolutely groundless, and would crave the indulgence of such owner and of my readers in general, while I endeavour to give my reasons for thinking so, since the subject is too important to be dismissed in a sentence.

First, then, let us assume for the sake of argument that the majority of the pheasants *do* fly away unharmed, which I am very far from thinking would actually be the case. What then? Some go on to Sir Timothy Markover's coverts, let us suppose, but why should they be wiped out? They might be, if he were shooting the same day, but this would be most unlikely to be the case.

Of the birds that have flown beyond the estate, some will

be back in their accustomed feeding place that evening, others in a day or two. A small proportion doubtless will not return at all, but what of that? Pheasants *will* stray, whether by the use of their legs or wings. Your neighbour gets some of your birds, you get some of his. So it's as broad as it's long. We are assuming, moreover, that all owners of pheasant coverts are in agreement about trying to show good birds. So a proportion of the tall birds missed by your neighbour's guests find their way into your coverts. One does not hear of the loss of birds from those owners of pheasant coverts who take a pride in showing good birds, and there are many such owners happily for the reputation of British sportsmanship.

As to the fear, often expressed, that good birds would be too good for most of the members, well, they might be. Especially if that particular syndicate were anything like the bookies' syndicate so amusingly described in Blackwood's magazine[1] a few years ago. But taking the average syndicate composed of retired members of the Services and professional and business men, bad shots are nowadays the exception rather than the rule. Thanks to shooting schools, the general standard of shooting has greatly improved during the last thirty or forty years. Few men in these days are so wealthy as to be willing to pay a large sum of money for the privilege of missing birds sent over them. Unless a man is a fairly good shot he eschews expensive shooting syndicates, preferring to devote his leisure to golf or some other pastime. But he may lack practice although a useful shot, and the very best practice he can have is afforded by high pheasants. It is a truism that the better the birds the better the shooting, so long as there are fair numbers of good birds to shoot at. It is your very occasional tall bird

[1] "Mixed Bagmen", by K. Stanford (*Blackwood's Magazine*, October 1939).

that is so often missed, just from lack of practice. But send them over in tolerable numbers and the guns soon begin to take toll of them.

Now, let us assume that a member—any member—of a shooting syndicate finds himself unable to deal satisfactorily with high pheasants—the average good bird coming well over the tree-tops. What does he do? What would anyone do in like case, who has just paid a biggish sum of money for the pleasure of shooting them? Would he not take the first opportunity of going to a shooting school, and practising at clays thrown from the high tower, with a good coach standing beside him to tell him what, and what not, to do? Of course he would, and two afternoons so spent should ensure his breaking two clays out of three. But it may be objected that clay pigeons are broken much easier than pheasants are killed, and this is perfectly true. High pheasants test the gun almost as much as they do the man behind it. He should see that his gun is sufficiently closely bored to throw a good pattern at forty yards with whatever size of shot he uses. A gun that is quite satisfactory on driven partridges may perform very badly indeed on high pheasants—a fact not always realised.

Assuming that the gun is correctly bored, a man who can make good practice on clays thrown from the 90-ft. tower, will assuredly perform well on high pheasants, unless these are so tall as to be almost out of range, and there are few places in England or Wales that can show such birds. A pheasant thirty yards high and going "all out" is a real good bird, and if our member can smash its clay imitation with fair consistency, he will not fail to take satisfactory toll of the real article.

Certainly, the free-wheeling high pheasant slanting downwards, and probably coming on a curve as well, will defeat any but a brilliant performer; but the average high bird will not be so exacting, and although the most difficult should always be attempted, the average shot may take comfort from this reflection.

In this connection it is worth noting that of all game-birds the tall pheasant can most successfully be imitated at shooting school by clay pigeons thrown from the high tower. One can easily overdo clay-pigeon shooting in practising at driven grouse or partridges, but for high pheasants one can hardly have too much of it. There is no question here of quick shooting. There is plenty of time to be deliberate, but it is very necessary to see that the clays are really coming over one at top speed.

Finally, so greatly are good pheasants appreciated even by those who have no scruples about shooting bad ones, that a shoot which consistently shows high pheasants very soon acquires a reputation; and the owner if really hampered by bad shots, can pick and choose his members for the next and subsequent seasons, for he will certainly not lack applications. I hope I have been able to make it clear that pheasants well shown, so far from being a liability, are a decided asset, alike to the owner of the coverts and to the members of the syndicate concerned, while the benefit to sport generally by the mere force of example is incalculable.

But the pleasantest form of syndicate—to use that objectionable word as applied to sport, for lack of a better one—is one composed of a small coterie of friends, three or four at most, who share expenses and the game; or by arrangement, agree to take a brace or two each at the end of the day's shooting, the bulk of the game being sold, and the proceeds credited to the shoot. Not only is this the pleasantest arrangement, but by far the cheapest. The man on the spot runs the shoot, that is to say, looks after the keeper or keepers, superintends the rearing

187

of pheasants and wild-duck (if any.), arranges the drives for partridges, and the beats for pheasants, and keeps the accounts. It is, of course, essential that he should be a methodical individual, and he cannot be too meticulous in the way he keeps the accounts, or too scrupulous about showing them to the other members at regular intervals, say once a month. His friends will probably say they don't want to be bothered, but he should insist nevertheless. It is only fair to them as well as to himself that they should see how their money is being spent.

The advantages of a shoot run on these lines are great. Each gun can ask a guest every time if he wants to, and there will be many occasions when a gun can ask two. Then, although the other members may live at a distance, all will take a real interest in the shoot, and will have a say in any question of importance, in which they would, as a matter of course, be consulted.

The keepers are the shoot's servants, and if the majority of the members disapprove of them, a change is promptly made. All the members draw for places together with their guests. There is no such thing, as so often happens in the ordinary syndicate shoot, of the owner of the coverts saying, as he presents the numbers to be drawn "I don't count", or "I don't draw, I am a rover—on the flank generally", or words to that effect. I have never quite been able to fathom why the manager of a syndicate, whether he owns the land or not, should not draw for places with everybody else. Whatever the reason, when the landowner running the shoot shares the chances of sport equally with the other members, his action is always noted and appreciated.

But to return to our shared shoot. Everything is settled by friendly discussion; the beaters' pay and their lunch, and whether a lunch is to be provided for the members and their guests, or whether each member is to bring his own. In the case of the shared shoot this is the simplest arrangement, and the best. An hour is amply long for any lunch, and gives the drivers or beaters, as the case may be, a good rest, and plenty of time for their dinner, which should be a hot stew if possible —a dish greatly appreciated on a cold winter's day. Syndicate shoots vary tremendously in this matter of lunch. Sometimes a very meagre one is supplied, unappetising to a degree. In others a most luxurious lunch is provided, lasting far too long —nearer two hours than one. In a short winter's day the best of the afternoon is gone before a shot is fired. It should not be difficult to find a happy mean between these two extremes. In a big syndicate shoot a general sit-down lunch is certainly desirable, making for geniality and good-fellowship among the members, but it should not be allowed to degenerate into a feast of Lucullus. One goes out to shoot, not to gorge, or absorb quantities of port.

The charm of the small shared shoot lies to a great extent in the absence of autocratic arrangements in which the members of a shooting syndicate have no voice. The proceedings, except for the drawing for places, are quite informal. Everyone is out to enjoy himself to the full. If birds are missed nobody cares. The shoot is the only loser, and that merely temporarily, for there will be all the more to shoot next time. Quality rather than quantity is the watchword where pheasants and wild-duck are concerned, and good relations with the farmers ensure, as far as possible, hedges being left untrimmed until the best of the partridge-driving is over. Unfortunately good ready-made shoots for letting seldom come into the market except by chance, and then at a very high rental; but it is sometimes possible to rent for a comparatively small sum very promising land for both partridges and pheasants, and there is never-failing interest in working up such a shoot, and seeing it improve year after year.

Fortunate indeed are the members of a small shoot who have succeeded in renting good partridge land, with some nice coverts for pheasants and perhaps water for wild-duck, and are able to look forward to an ever-improving shoot after the first year. While he is waiting for things to develop, a member might do worse than join for one season a big syndicate shoot if he can afford it. He may pick up some useful tips both on the positive and negative side, and it will be strange if his experiences do not enhance the joy of possession of his own little shoot, shared though it be (and none the worse for that) with all the possibilities it presents.

On re-reading these pages, I am conscious of having been unintentionally a little hard on the owners of syndicate shoots. But I had in mind chiefly those owners whose chief concern it is to rake in the shekels irrespective of the sport shown. For such as these I have little sympathy. But for the other sort who, while hoping to cover their expenses and come out on the right side, lay themselves out to show their guests the best sport available I have every sympathy, as indeed we must all have. For they have a great deal to put up with. For one reason or another it is inevitable that a certain number of the guns must be new each season, and these are more or less an unpredictable quantity. One member may be a greedy shot, given to firing at anything within range regardless of whether it was his bird or his neighbour's. Another may be dangerous; and yet another, having paid the price of two guns in the shoot, may consider that this entitles him to run it chiefly with an eye to his own advantage. This sportsman may be difficult to deal with, particularly if he is elderly, since the enhanced price will probably come as a godsend to the impoverished owner, and he

190

may, therefore, have to walk as delicately as Agag, for a time at least, in order not to offend his "important" guest who is only too well aware of the fact. The owner of a syndicate shoot may consider himself fortunate indeed if all his members are sportsmen in the true sense of the word and pleasant fellows to boot.

Then there is the perennial difficulty in finding beaters, and in these days of strikes and industrial unrest the keeper will be lucky if he can count on two or three reliable old hands to leaven the mass of rag-tag and bobtail which perforce he has had to rope in. And the pay may vary, and probably will, from season to season, always with a tendency to increase.

In short the manager of a syndicate shoot in the most favourable circumstances has much cause for anxiety; while if the syndicate is not a happy family, or if things go wrong, he is a man greatly to be pitied. In any case he needs all the help he can get from his members in the shape of tact, punctuality, and decent behaviour. On the other hand, the members, having paid their money, are entitled to a fair deal and due consideration. It is when the scales are evenly balanced that the syndicate shoot comes into its own.

CHANGED CONDITIONS

The syndicate? Does it flourish still?
    Or is it now beneath the weather?
Shall we desire to test our skill,
    As once, on driven fur and feather?

Or when we sadly estimate
    The state of our depleted coffers
Must we decline to contemplate
    A syndicate's attractive offers?

And seek instead, through journeys wide,
    With small expenditure of cash
To rent land likely to provide
    A hunting ground for Don or Dash,

And share it with another gun,
    As more agreeable (and cheaper),
And work it up, and have our fun
    With each of us his own gamekeeper?

WELL RETRIEVED

STEADY TO SHOT

CHAPTER XX

DOGS (1)

The all-round gun-dog

IT IS NOT PROPOSED here to treat of the various breeds of
sporting dogs at large, but rather to discuss the type of dog
best suited to the needs of the one-dog man. This will naturally depend on the kind of shooting he goes in for. If he is the
owner of a rough shoot where the game consists chiefly of
rabbits, with a sprinkling of wild pheasants and an occasional
covey of partridges, undoubtedly a spaniel is the most suitable
dog, and he can please himself as to the particular breed of
spaniel he fancies. A cocker—not the show type—is very
useful for turning out rabbits from gorse and brambles which
would defeat a larger dog. It is, however, usually too small to
retrieve a cock pheasant cleanly, but will generally manage to
drag it out of a hedge or thicket and hold it until its master
comes to the rescue.

The Devonshire spaniel, which is little bigger than a large-
sized cocker, is another useful type of spaniel for a rough
shoot. Whatever the breed it must work within shot. This is
largely but not entirely a matter of training. Spaniels as a

breed are inclined to be wild, and some are so headstrong that despite careful training as a puppy nothing can be done with them. A great advantage of the cocker is that it makes a perfect house-dog, but unfortunately is often spoiled in the process. Fortunately, many dogs if they have been accustomed to being isolated from puppyhood do not mind being shut up alone. Others are miserable, and evince it by piteous howlings. A dog that from boisterous habits is unsuited to the house, and at the same time is miserable when shut up alone is best got rid of.

Then there is the shooter who does a good deal of rough shooting, but also belongs to a shooting syndicate which has some grouse or partridge driving, and pheasant coverts as well. He really requires two types of dog. A spaniel of some kind for his rough shoot, and a well-broken retriever for the butts and the covert side. The only spaniel I have personally known that would hunt game, and at the same time be perfectly steady and non-slip during a grouse or partridge drive, was a cross-bred Clumber with a good deal of setter in him. No beauty to look at, but full of sense. The Labrador retriever —most charming of dogs—also makes a good compromise, but it is rather asking for trouble to let a well-broken retriever do spaniel's work in addition to its own. The risk of making it unsteady is great, especially when it is used to push rabbits out of cover. Nearly all retrievers make good house-dogs and companions, and I have never known a Labrador that did not.

Again there is the man whose chief quarry is the snipe, and who pursues that elusive bird over moor and mountain, meadow and bog. He will require a setter or pointer for the moor, and indeed more than one if he does a good deal of dogging for grouse. But the owner of a grouse-moor on which dogs are used to find the game would naturally have a kennel

194

of setters or pointers, and we are here concerned with the one-dog man. To return to the snipe. The best breed of dog for this sport would depend on whether the snipe-shooter's wanderings took him chiefly over moor and mountain, and the large bogs of the west of Ireland, or whether he confined himself chiefly to water meadows and small bogs. For work on a moor a good steady setter is essential. The pointer may be ruled out. It is not fair to work a thin-coated dog over the wet ground on which snipe are found. Moreover, the average pointer is not as companionable as a setter, and does not as a rule make a good house-dog. There are, of course, exceptions, and a pointer I once owned was as companionable a dog as one could wish for.

There is no reason why a setter should not be taught to retrieve. I have not found that this makes them unsteady on point, but it does, I think, incline them to run in to the fall of game. This, however, is not of great importance to the snipe-shooter, particularly as a sensible dog soon gives up chasing, realising the futility of it. A dog that runs in every time a snipe gets up is, of course, an intolerable nuisance, but this is generally a fault of puppyhood, and is easily checked, unless the dog is naturally wild and headstrong, in which case the sooner it is got rid of the better. If a setter has been taught to keep to heel, it can be taken over any sort of snipe ground, and used as a retriever pure and simple. But it is really rather too big for this sort of work, and is bound very often by splashing to alarm snipe on bogs and marshy ground.

The best dog I ever saw as a retriever on snipe was a diminutive cocker bitch. She had, I think, been very severely trained, and was not well cared for. Her coat was in a dreadful state, and her quarters were in a dirty stable on a bed of musty straw. But over rushy meadows where her owner chiefly used her she was *facile princeps*. She never left his heel till sent forward when a snipe was down. In a fever of suppressed excitement when walking along a road she would run continually from one of her master's heels to the other, never forging in front, and with her nose always on one heel or the other. At every step, from right to left and vice versa the little dog went continuously, a curious trick which must have been acquired as a puppy. I never heard her master say a kind word to her, or saw him take any notice of her, except to signal her forward to retrieve a snipe. She had a beautiful nose and invariably found her bird. This little cocker was a most useful ally, for she was so small, and followed so closely, that her owner could take her anywhere, secure in the knowledge that she was practically noiseless.

Cockers, like most spaniels, are inclined to be impetuous until old age has sobered them, and very few could be trained to the degree above recorded. Probably the dog best suited to the solitary snipe-shooter on fens and marshes, as distinct from large bogs and moors, would be a well-broken Irish water spaniel, or a small hard-coated retriever of the Labrador type, or possibly a spaniel with a good deal of Clumber blood in it. I advocate a cross-breed rather than pure Clumber as Clumbers are low on the leg, and in consequence, easily tire, and moreover carry very thick coats; also they are delicate dogs and often rather morose in temperament. But of all the various breeds of spaniel they are the quietest, and in intelligence second to none.

For the snipe-shooter who frequents moors and mountains as much as, or even more than, he does the rushy bottoms, a steady retrieving setter can hardly be beaten.

I always feel sorry for pointers. Their sporting joys are so few and far between, compared with those of other breeds.

196

Their usefulness is limited, in these islands at any rate, to two short months at most, for grouse will not stand to dogs as a rule after the end of September. On the Continent where they train pointers to retrieve they can be used for a much longer period. The unfortunate pointer, too, is usually relegated to a kennel, and has a dismal time unless it be one of a number of dogs; frequently both its constitution and temper are ruined from lack of exercise.

The setter, on the other hand, if it belongs to the one-dog man, has a much better time as a rule, for it makes a delightful companion, and in consequence is usually made free of the house and grounds. It is, therefore, never dull, as a dog must be when shut up in a kennel for hours on end. If, moreover, it is trained to retrieve, its sporting days are considerably extended, for it can be used as a retriever on all kinds of shooting: setters have occasionally been known to beat retrievers proper at their own game.

As to the different breeds of setters, like most of us I have my personal preference, but refrain from naming it, since to do so would serve no useful purpose. I have tried most breeds and have found good in all, except in the show specimens, which, like the show cockers, have usually had all the brains bred out of them.

THE ALL-ROUNDER

The all-round dog should have a nose
Improving as he older grows;
And if he's troubled with "the slows"
   Perhaps 'tis just as well.

He should be biddable and bold,
Keep patiently to heel till told
To follow scent, now hot, now cold,
   Through brambly copse or dell.

Persistent he should be and wise,
Quite free from chase, yet use his eyes
To watch a bird that stricken flies,
   And mark the spot it fell.

What profits it to cavil o'er
A spaniel or a Labrador?
A treasure yours more choice than ore
   Can buy, or tongue can tell.

CHAPTER XXI

DOGS (2)

Notes on training and Kennel Management

FOR SOME TIME I thought of embodying in this chapter
detailed instructions as to the training of young puppies in
their first lessons, but ultimately decided against it for two good
and sufficient reasons. First, because anything I could say has
already been better said by several authorities with far greater
experience of dogs than I can lay claim to. Second, in writing
of training dogs—I hate the word breaking—it is, I find,
extremely difficult to shut off each lesson into a separate water-
tight compartment, as it were. If every puppy were born with
the same temperament this would be easy enough. But one
cannot, beyond a point, train dogs by rule of thumb, so that in
giving directions one cannot say, "do this, that, or the other,
and success will follow." No one knows whether it will or
not, until he or she has made personal trial of it. There must,
therefore, necessarily be a good many "ifs", and it is the "ifs"
that constitute the stumbling block. Without them, in a subject

such as this, directions are not of much use; with them they become too lengthy for a chapter, or indeed for two, and it is understandable, therefore, why people who have written comprehensively on the training of even one kind of gun-dog have needed a whole book for their subject.

To start at the very beginning the question arises as to the best time to buy a puppy. Here the intending purchaser of a likely puppy is in something of a quandary. Puppies born in autumn and winter, not later than January, can be worked in the following shooting season. Spring puppies, of course, cannot. On the other hand, autumn and winter puppies have to face the cold and damp of early spring and winter at the time their constitutions are weakest, from two to four months (the weather is immaterial until after the puppies are weaned). But they have this great advantage over puppies born in the spring, that their education can proceed without check, particularly in the later stages, right up to and including the shooting season, whereas the training of spring puppies after the first two or three months is subject to constant interruptions, in proportion as the shooting season makes demands on the time of the owner, or his gamekeeper, unless a large kennel with a trainer is part of the establishment. Too young to take any part in the shooting season, the advanced training of spring puppies must necessarily suffer neglect till February, and then nothing can be shot over them until August or September comes round, except rabbits or an occasional pigeon.

Probably if one could choose the month, a puppy born late in December or early in January would be the one to buy. However, the chances are that matters will be arranged by Dame Nature without any consideration for the wishes or convenience of the purchaser, who must either buy when he can or lose an opportunity of acquiring a puppy from selected

200

parents, possibly field trial winners. Still, I would not personally buy a puppy born in the spring or summer if I could afford
to wait.

Having decided on the litter from which the purchase is to
be made, the next consideration is the age at which to buy.
Here again I can only state my own predilection. For every
reason, I believe in taking the puppy soon after it is weaned,
at about two months old. It is a risk, of course, but no greater
than in leaving it possibly to have fits about which one may
hear nothing, or, if bought from strangers, to be injudiciously
fed and allowed to pick up garbage, a habit which, if acquired
as a small puppy, is very difficult to eradicate. Also I am a
believer in giving the early lessons at an early age. The puppy
should be inoculated against distemper as soon as it is old
enough.

In choosing a puppy the advice as to picking a bold one is
undoubtedly sound. A nervous puppy is likely to be a constant source of trouble, liable to develop gun-shyness, and
later to be attacked by that mysterious disease, canine hysteria.
But besides boldness, intelligence and docility are needed. It
is doubtful whether the advice of the late Mr. W. Arkwright[1]
on choosing a puppy can be bettered. He says, "Firstly, then,
as to the pup's actual pedigree, he should have a first-rate
dam; one that excels in natural talent, one, if possible, that is
the favourite shooting companion of her master. His sire's
excellence there is not quite so much necessity to investigate;
for one reason because the owner of a good bitch will almost
certainly have exercised care in her mating.

"Secondly," he goes on, "choose from the litter a puppy
with a big round skull well filled over the temples, and a look
of dauntless curiosity in his well-opened eyes. See that he

[1] Introduction to *Spaniels: their breaking for Sport and Field Trials.*

does not run back from your inspection to hide himself under the straw; see that on being handled he does not make water which is a sure sign of nerves morbidly developed. Nerves in excess are a nuisance, and are to be dreaded quite as much as a lazy and phlegmatic disposition."

To the above I would only add that, after their first exuberance was over, my choice, other things being equal, would fall on a puppy that, with head on one side and wrinkled brow, regarded one with a look of puzzled attention, as if trying to understand what one was saying. Even at this early age such an expression denotes docility and sense, and the chances are all in favour of the selection turning out an apt pupil.

I have a prejudice against a light-coloured eye in a gun-dog, as I think it indicates a flighty disposition, and it is certainly ugly. A dark-brown or hazel eye is the colour most in keeping with a handsome specimen of any breed.

As to training, I think one can hardly begin too early in giving the first lessons—lessons, that is, which do not tax the puppy's brain or strength in any way, but merely encourage docility and obedience. These can often be combined without confusing the puppy in the slightest degree. The first thing, of course, is to establish friendly relations, and to get the puppy to regard its owner as its master to the exclusion—more or less, since it is only a small puppy—of other people. Cupboard love, of course, but soon to be followed by real affection. Having got so far, one of the first lessons should be to teach it to come to whistle at a gallop. This presents no difficulty if at first a tit-bit is always kept handy, but it should be practised whenever the puppy is exercised. It may now receive its first lessons in retrieving. If all goes well, later lessons can at discretion be deferred until the puppy gets bigger and stronger. But it is a great thing to know that one has a potential retriever, and this cannot be discovered without a trial. Most well-bred puppies from retrieving stock pick up the object straight away, and come "galumphing" after one as fast as their short legs and fat body will let them.

Puppies should be accustomed to the report of a gun at the earliest age. Anything at feeding time can be used at first, that will make a report similar to and as loud as a gun-shot. The firer begins at a distance, firing half a dozen shots, and daily coming closer according as the puppies react. Finally, hardly a puppy will trouble to lift its nose from the dish, even when the gun is fired almost over them. A morbidly nervous puppy might be put off its feed, but I have never seen this happen when the firing has begun far off, and when the distance has been gradually decreased. This practice usually takes about a week, but should be continued until all fear of gun-shyness is at an end.

Dropping to hand can be combined with the other lessons. When I say combined, I mean that it should form part of the daily curriculum. It can, as a matter of fact, actually be combined with early lessons in retrieving, for when the puppy has learnt to drop at the uplifted hand and word of command, it is very useful to drop it to start with when it is being taught not to retrieve until ordered to do so. For the early lessons in dropping to hand, retrieving, and keeping to heel, the puppy should trail a light cord, not longer than three yards at first.

This brings me to the last of the early lessons, but by no means the least important, keeping to heel. Several authorities are in favour of deferring this lesson to the last on the ground that repression is bad for the puppy's soul, tending to check boldness, and to turn it into a spiritless automaton. It has also been advanced that it is harmful to a puppy's initiative, and prevents it from acquiring the wisdom gained from various experiences and an investigating nose. I can only say that speaking from my own experience I have not found this to be the case. To begin with there is frequently no repression at all, and if any is needed it is of so slight a nature as not to harm the puppy in any way. Strange as it may seem in an active creature like a dog, many puppies seem to enjoy keeping to heel, if they have been used to it from the time they were small. For the matter of that, most dogs enjoy a ride in a cart or a motor car, when one might suppose they would be horribly bored. Pace has nothing to do with it, for they are just as happy when the vehicle, whatever it may be, is moving at five miles an hour as at fifty.

As to checking initiative, the puppy is only kept to heel for comparatively short periods, and has unlimited opportunities of acquiring wisdom during exercise, and in the course of training. On the other hand, when a puppy has been allowed to run free practically unchecked up to six months of age or even over, a great deal of repression is generally required before it can be made consistently to remain at heel till signalled forward. What is learnt as a small puppy becomes second nature, and if obedience can be taught and absorbed at an early age, it is far less likely to do harm than if it has to be hammered into a strong and well-grown dog used to going where it likes, investigating rabbit holes and what not, and occasionally indulging in the delights of a rabbit hunt. To such a dog keeping at heel must necessarily be irksome, for it is always wanting to break away at every passing distraction of scent, sight, or sound.

A great advantage in teaching a young puppy to keep to heel is that it can be taken anywhere, and the more a puppy is with one the more it learns. A puppy of any breed that will come to whistle at a gallop, keep at heel till ordered forward, and drop to hand and remain dropped until released, is an acquisition; for a sound foundation has been built up on which all subsequent training will rest. There is no question here of overbreaking, for lessons in obedience have been acquired unconsciously and with a minimum of restraint. I have never yet seen a sensible puppy spoiled from early lessons in keeping to heel, and never expect to. The trainer must, of course, use his discrimination. Some puppies take naturally to keeping to heel at an early age. For those which do not the lesson may be deferred until the puppy is from 3 to 4 months old.

Before leaving the subject of keeping to heel, it may be as well to say that to keep a puppy at heel for two or three minutes only is useless. If kept at heel for such a short time it gets into the way of expecting the releasing order at any moment, and before long is extremely likely to anticipate it. After allowing it to work off its exuberance, the puppy should be kept at heel for at least ten minutes. The walks should be varied as much as possible, moor, open fields, woods, roads, paths and streets being traversed in turn as opportunity permits. At this stage the more the puppy is introduced to cattle, horses, sheep, poultry, hares and humans, and taught to ignore them the better.

After ten minutes or a quarter of an hour at heel, the puppy may be waved forward, and allowed to romp and otherwise amuse itself, but the lesson should end with the puppy once more at heel on the return to the house.

A few remarks on training generally for the benefit of the novice may not be out of place.

At first the lessons should be as short as possible, but they should be regularly practised. From five to ten minutes is quite long enough for any lesson in the early stages; some, indeed, as for instance coming to whistle, or retrieving a dummy, may take but a minute. A lesson should not be repeated more than twice or three times at most, and not practised oftener than twice a day. The first time a new lesson is taught, if all goes well, any repetition at the time is best postponed. The object to aim at is always to finish up with a successful attempt, even if it is only partial. The risk of boring the puppy is to be avoided at all costs. In continuity and un-failing patience lies the main secret of success, if secret there be.

As regards the more advanced training, there are one or two points which seem to call for remark here. The first is the practice often seen of beating a young dog for chasing or running in to shot. Another is working a setter or pointer for too long at a time. This applies to any young dog, but par-ticularly to the breeds mentioned.

To beat a dog, young or old, for determined chasing or running-in is cruel, and useless in nine cases out of ten. One might go so far as to say in ninety-nine cases in a hundred. What has happened is that the centuries-old inherited instinct of the wild has overmastered the newly-acquired habit of obedience. Nature versus discipline, in fact. The dog should be rated, certainly, on its return, if only to show it that its excursions are disapproved of, but beaten, no. The cure is the checkcord, which, if judiciously used, is most effective, especi-ally if an element of surprise can be introduced. In fact this must be managed somehow. But see that the checkcord is sufficiently strong to hold the impetuous rush of a strong well-grown puppy, which should not only be checked, but, if possible, turned completely over, for it is the sudden and unexpected shock coming in mid-career which has such beneficial results. One or two lessons of the kind will cure the most inveterate runner-in, when beating would be utterly useless.

Here we may consider the difficult question of how to treat rabbits. Should they be ignored, or should the young dog be allowed to retrieve them? I think it depends largely on the kind of dog being trained. If a setter, pointer, or even retriever, rabbits are best left alone, and any inclination on the part of a puppy to chase them sternly repressed—a comparatively easy task with these breeds. But if a spaniel, which incidentally should always be taught to retrieve, is the pupil, its job in a rough shoot will be more concerned with rabbits than with anything else. It has to push them out of thick stuff, and retrieve them when shot. So the more it sees of them in puppyhood the better. But not to chase them. The checkcord is the only adequate preventive known to the writer and, as before stated, it must come as a surprise.

At this stage a capable assistant is virtually a necessity. Let the trainer, accompanied by a keeper or other person with a gun, take the puppy, by now probably 5 or 6 months old, to a place where rabbits are certain to be found. He will previously have fixed a long checkcord of some 25 yards in length to its collar. The puppy will have been used to trailing a checkcord of from 3 to 20 yards at various stages in its training. A rabbit can either be poked out of a thicket, or be come upon when in the open on a summer's evening. Wherever found it must be arranged that it is shot, and that the dog sees it shot. If shot as it is bolting so much the better. The puppy will previously have been ordered to heel, but the spectacle of a bolting bunny turning a somersault in response to a well-directed shot in the head will be too much for youthful canine nature. Instantly it will be in full pursuit, but the trainer picks up the end of the cord, and as the puppy reaches the limit, shouts "No", and braces himself to meet the sudden strain. This time it is the puppy that turns head-over-heels.

When it finds its feet again it is called to heel, but otherwise no notice is taken of it. Presently with the puppy at heel the trainer strolls to the dead rabbit, and picks it up, not letting the dog touch it or even smell it, and hands it to the assistant. The puppy should be taken straight home, and the lesson repeated at the end of ten days when the previous one may have been partially forgotten.

The checkcord defeats its object unless the puppy is going all out, for the shock should be associated in the dog's mind with the stern "No" of his master, rather than with the cord, which it has trailed without any unpleasant associations off and on since it was three months old.

A word of caution may perhaps be advisable here. First, the checkcord, while strong enough to stand the sudden strain to which it will be subjected, must not be so heavy as to be an impediment to the galloping puppy. If too heavy it will slow the dog up, and the lesson will be thrown away, since the puppy will only feel a slight check, and be quite ready to run in and mouth the rabbit as soon as released. On the other hand, if not strong enough, the cord will break at the critical moment, and this will be pure disaster; for the released puppy will rush in and worry the rabbit to its heart's content, and weeks of careful training will be undone in a matter of seconds. So weight and breaking strain should be given careful consideration when the cord is purchased.

The trainer can, of course, step on the cord instead of lifting it, but this is risky. It may be pulled from under his foot, or it may upset him if the puppy should be a half-grown Labrador, or dog of that weight. Far better to leave nothing to chance.

As a matter of fact, if a dog used for rough shooting only runs in to the fall of game it is often an advantage rather than otherwise. An intelligent dog soon learns to use its brains in this respect, and many a winged cock pheasant or duck which would otherwise be lost finds a place in the bag thanks to good marking and instant pursuit on the part of the dog. But for driven game and covert-shooting steadiness is essential, and in any case these early lessons with the checkcord will prevent the chase of unshot-at ground-game, which otherwise would continue as a habit to the end of the chapter.

In all cases of disobedience on the part of dogs, if the offender can be surprised in the act, the application of a sudden shock of however mild a nature has an infinitely better effect than a dozen beatings after the offence has been committed. Corporal punishment for offences of instinct, as distinct from acts of deliberate disobedience, is not only futile, but destroys a dog's self-respect, rendering it sulky or shy according to its nature, and is very likely to cow it. But surprise it in the act, and the effect is astonishing.

A common instance is the case of a well-fed puppy that has acquired the habit of picking up garbage. Ratings and beatings after the offence has been committed are quite useless. The moment your back is turned it will be off to the dust heap or other delectable spot again. But if you steal up to it while it is poking about and is quite unaware of your presence, and deal a smart cut with a whip or supple ash-plant, at the same time rapping out an emphatic "No", it will jump nearly out of its skin and flee with a yelp of dismay. One or two surprises of the kind will most probably effect a cure, whereas in spite of ratings and beatings it would otherwise continue to hunt for and pick up garbage to the end of the chapter. Naturally, before attempting surprises of the kind suggested, one would make quite certain that the puppy was being judiciously fed, and was free from worms.

The bad habit of garbage-hunting in well cared for puppies

can often be traced to their having been allowed to forage for themselves from the time they were weaned, until they came under proper control.

Many young setters and pointers are spoiled every season by being worked too long at a time, especially under a hot August sun. From 1 to 1½ hours is ample for a young dog, and it should then be taken up for the day. It should, of course, gradually be hardened before being worked on a moor. A tired dog is very apt to become a potterer, and I think very often frequent false pointing can be attributed to this cause.

As regards retrievers, he is a wise man who in his dog's first season makes his shooting subservient to its education. This is asking much of human nature, but not too much from the man who is the fortunate possessor of a puppy likely to turn out first-class, and who perhaps has given months of patient work to training it. Let him forego shooting for a day or two when dogging is in progress on a grouse-moor, or birds are being walked up. He will be well repaid in the long run by following with his young retriever at heel, and allowing it to retrieve an occasional dead bird.

The less a young dog sees of grouse-butts the better. The presence of other dogs, perhaps not all well trained, is demoralising, and still more so is the sight of birds dropping round him. If a young dog is taken into a butt as an experience it should either be held by an attendant while its master is shooting, or securely tethered to a tuft of heather, or to a spike driven into the ground. Should it break loose months of patient work will probably be ruined in five minutes. Exactly the same thing applies when shooting driven partridges. An occasional experience will do the young dog no harm, always provided that adequate measures are taken against the possibility of its getting loose, and that it is only allowed to retrieve an occasional dead bird, and preferably one that requires finding.

Far better is it to give the puppy practice in sitting by its master while the latter is waiting for wildfowl to flight, or for wood pigeons coming in to roost. In both these pursuits a measure of attention can be given to the dog that could never be spared for a moment while shooting driven grouse or partridges. Not until a dog can be trusted to sit by its master for an indefinite time without moving, regardless of temptation, is it fit to be taken into a grouse-butt or to a partridge-stand, unless held or tied.

As already indicated in these pages I am no believer in relegating a single dog to a kennel. I think a puppy treated as a house-dog has opportunities of acquiring wisdom denied to the other. There is no reason why it should be spoiled, if only it can be kept away from children, who will ruin any puppy. The only other objection that I can see to keeping a sensible gun-dog puppy in the house is that it is apt to lie too much in front of the fire in winter. This does not appear to do any harm if, as it should, it gets a lot of out-door exercise. It is not always realised that there are bad draughts underneath doors, and the puppy should be trained to sleep on a raised bench or basket according to its size. In the dining-room it should not be allowed to prowl round the room at meal-times and make itself a nuisance, but should have a corner out of the draught allotted to it, and be made to lie there until the meal is over.

With regard to ailments, the dog is a hardy animal if not inbred, and with ordinary care is seldom ill. With puppies the most critical time is from two to four months. Teething trouble, which sometimes is the cause of fits, is over at five months or shortly after, and although distemper may occur at any age it is more likely to attack a puppy between two and four months than at any other time. Short of infection there is no reason why healthy puppies should get distemper. Nevertheless inoculation is a wise precaution.

Practically all puppies, and most dogs, suffer from worms, puppies from roundworms, and full-grown dogs usually, but not always, from tapeworm. Puppies often acquire worms from the dam's milk. Worms are a frequent cause of fits and other ailments, and must be got rid of or the puppies will never thrive. They should be periodically dosed from the time they are eight weeks old. For puppies, santonin in castor-oil is as good as anything, the dose being graduated according to the age and breed of the puppies. "Ruby" mixture is also excellent for puppies. For full-grown dogs I have found Naldire's worm powders excellent, if one can be certain of getting them fresh. If not fresh they are very likely to be inoperative. If there is any doubt about it, it is best to get the areca nut, and grate off the required amount, with a coarse rasp, in the proportion of one grain to a pound of the dog's weight. All dogs should be dosed twice a year for worms, irrespective of whether they show signs of them or not. Spring and autumn are convenient times of year. Only by periodical dosing can one be sure of keeping dogs free from these pests.

Canker of the ear is a very common ailment, particularly in long-eared dogs, and those that go much into water. Fortunately, if taken in time, it is a very easy complaint to treat. The ear should first be thoroughly but gently cleaned by swabs of cotton wool wound round a stick of the thickness of a pencil and dipped in half a tumbler of warm water, to which a tablespoonful of methylated spirit has been added. The ear should then be well dried by dry cotton wool used in the same manner.

After this, pour a teaspoonful of boracic acid powder well into the ear, and gently manipulate the base of the ear until the powder has worked right down. If canker has been neglected more drastic remedies will be needed, and it may be very difficult to cure.

Canine hysteria is a comparatively modern disease and scientists have not yet discovered what causes it. Whether it is on the increase or the reverse I do not know, but unfortunately it is common enough. Undue excitement and fatigue, particularly on a warm day, may bring on an attack, and there is no doubt that injudicious feeding is a contributory cause. Any derangement of the intestines, particularly constipation, is very liable to end in an attack, and nervous and excitable dogs are more prone to it than those of a placid disposition. Some bacteriologists think that it is due to parasites in the inner ear, a further reason for treating canker as soon as it appears. Certainly the last dog of mine to have hysteria had slight canker of the ear, but what actually brought on the seizure was a mad chase after a hare following on a hard morning's work. The dog returned completely exhausted, and an attack followed almost immediately.

Hysteria invariably comes on suddenly. The dog is seen to stand still and look round in a dazed fashion. It then commences to bark and dashes off in any direction. It is for the time being quite blind and perfectly unconscious. It runs into any obstacle in its path, tries to climb walls, or rushes into some dark corner. It has not the faintest notion of where it is going or what it is doing. The puppy I have mentioned—it was just a year old—rammed its head into a peat bog. It then fell over, and when I got up to it, its nostrils and mouth were completely blocked with black slimy peat. But for timely assistance the dog must shortly have died from suffocation. Ten minutes later it had a second fit, but it was now on a lead, and it was possible, although difficult, to restrain it. Fortunately water was conveniently handy, and thoroughly wetting the back of its head brought it to, and it was at once taken home in the car and treated. That was some months ago, and it has never had another attack.

Treatment is simple, although a permanent cure is by no means assured. Entire rest for a fortnight or three weeks in a warm and dry kennel; in a darkened room for three or four days, with small doses of bromide two or three times a day for a week or ten days. One must be careful, however, not to overdo the bromide, as the effect of too frequent doses is to stupefy the dog, and ultimately to affect its brain. The dog should have opening medicine and be kept on a milk diet— bread and milk, milk puddings, etc., three times a day for ten days at least, gradually returning to the normal diet. No exercise for at least a fortnight, and then it should be very gradually resumed.

As to the general treatment of gun-dogs, they should be housed in dry and well-ventilated kennels, draught-proof, and giving access to sun and air. There should be a platform on which the dog can bask in sunny weather, with the actual sleeping place in the shade. The bedding should be changed once a week in winter and twice weekly in summer. Every dog should be brushed once daily. It only takes a couple of minutes for each dog, and keeps the coat in splendid order. It is of the first importance that a dog should never be put into its kennel wet. It should always be well dried first, and chamois leather is the only article I know of that will dry a long-coated dog such as a setter or spaniel. After most of the wet has been got off with the "chammy", a good rub with a hard towel will do the rest. When going shooting I always take a "chammy" leather and a couple of towels in the car, and see that the dog is well dried before the journey home is begun.

As regards diet, I believe in variety with a fair allowance of meat for a carnivorous animal, especially after a hard day's work. From six months to a year a dog should have two meals a day; afterwards it will depend on the animal's constitution. Some do best with only one meal, for others, two is a necessity. In any case the first meal should be a light one—porridge and milk or something similar. Dog biscuit alone is not suitable as a staple diet. It is too starchy, and is generally lacking in essential vitamins, but is excellent when mixed with meat and vegetables. Green vegetables and potatoes in their jackets are good if the dog will eat them mixed with meat; so are crusts of whole-meal bread baked in the oven to a crisp consistency, and given with a minimum of soup to flavour them. Fish when available makes a much appreciated change, and rabbit as a regular standby cannot be beaten. Care should be taken not to overfeed. It is better to give too little than too much.

Bones, preferably raw, should be large and given with circumspection, and never by any chance to a dog when in its kennel, or it will crunch them on its bedding, and in the process absorb quite a lot of straw or shavings, to the detriment of its internal organs. Even the most intelligent dogs appear to have no discrimination in these matters. Bones taken on to bedding are a fruitful source of constipation with its attendant evils.

Daily exercise is, of course, essential, and can hardly be overdone. The cruelty of keeping an active animal like a dog shut up in its kennel, or chained in a yard for days together cannot always be realised, or it would not be as common as it is in these so-called enlightened days.

The shooter who is the fortunate owner of a really good dog which he has himself trained, possesses a faithful ally capable of enhancing tenfold the pleasure of his shooting, and a devoted companion at all times. The least he can do, then, is to bestow on it the care and attention necessary to keep it in good health, and ensure for it a modicum of contentment in the dull days of the close season.

THE TREASURE

If you can breed or buy or beg a puppy
    Whose parents are of well-known sporting strain,
      And have patience, time and ground
      In which to train your likely hound,
    You'll be working for immeasurable gain.

Not in terms of L.S.D., you understand,
    But in treasure that is worth its weight in gold;
      For your pup may have a nose
      That improves the more it grows,
    And be biddable, and sensible, and bold.

In short, you may acquire the perfect gun-dog,
    Or, conversely, it may prove a perfect dud;
      Notwithstanding careful breeding
      It may not be worth its feeding,
    And be useless for the purposes of stud.

Or your treasured pup may meet with fatal illness
    From distemper, or hysteria, or germs;
      Or a car around the corner
      May convert you to a mourner,
    And your prospects to a mangled heap of worms.

And altho' it's hardly likely at the outset
    That success your early efforts will attend,
      Yet if patience be enrolled,
      And your temper well controlled,
    Success will surely greet you in the end.

Then indeed you'll have a treasure worth the guarding
Who'll adapt itself to all your trying ways;
Who'll adore you as a god,
And obey your slightest nod,
And enhance a hundredfold your shooting days.

Then here's a health to all our good companions,
To Peter, Punch, or Nell, the perfect gem;
May we cherish them with kindness,
And (not spoiling them in blindness)
May we pay back half the debt we owe to them!

ENVOI

Time was when I could walk for hours together,
   And hold my own among my sporting peers,
And realised, in spite of wind and weather,
   Shots without tears.

Whether I walked up grouse in knee-deep heather,
   Or tramped to points of setters ranging wide,
Or ploughed through bogs, or hunted fur and feather
   On the hill-side,

Or stood in butts in keen anticipation
   Of distant grouse the size of bumble-bees
Advancing rapidly to decimation,
   Helped by the breeze,

I had my fun; but now my figure's portly,
   My sight less keen, while as for wind I've none;
Yet memories of past delights have brought me
   To carry on.

And though Jones of a younger generation
   With scornful smile is often standing by
To take my birds, and without hesitation
   To wipe my eye,

There still remains a final consolation,
   Triumph by proxy so to me it seems;
I can at least defeat with devastation
   Jones in my dreams.

INDEX

221